An Introduction to Selling

By
Larry Yslas

Table of Contents

Part One: Introduction 1

The Purpose of This Book 2
The Definition of Selling 4
A Background Profile of Selling 6
Myths About Selling 9
What to Expect as You Read This Book 11

Part Two: The Basic Elements 13

Element One
The Product or Service 14
Know Your Product or Service 15
A Partial, but Effective, List of Things to Know 16
How To Select A Product or Service 18

Element Two
Buyers 21
Know Your Buyers 22
Another Partial List Of Things To Know 23
Generating Buyers 24
Indirect Methods 26
Direct Methods 28
A Few Methods of Prospecting 31
How to Approach Buyers 34
Qualifying Buyers 35

Element Three
Motives 38

Element Four
Price 42

Element Five
Decisions, the Core of the Sale 44
Why Getting Decisions is Difficult............................. 44
Decision Making is a Process 45
How to Get Decisions 47
Closing 47
The Dreaded Topic of Objections............................... 50
Some Closing Techniques... 52
Steps to Effective Closing... 55
Buyer's Remorse... 56

Special Considerations 58

Skills 58
The Big 10 Percent.. 59
Time & Timing 60
Fears 62

Part Three: Tools Of The Trade.................................. 64

Organization.. 65
How To Organize.. 67
Planning 69
Numbers.. 72
Listening 74
Observation... 77

Telephones	79
Questions	81
Negotiating	83
Thinking	85
Intuition	87
Words	88
Body Language	91
Service	92
Stories	96
Analogies	98
Visual Aids	100
Methods	101
Persuasion	103
Scripting	104
The Voice	107
Communications	109

Part Four: The Sixth Basic Element 111

Sellers	111
A Career in Selling	112
Goals	119
Self Image	122
Professionalism	123
Money	125
Appearance and Grooming	126
Studying	128
Ethics	128
Work Habits	130
Manners	130
Attitude	131

PART ONE

INTRODUCTION

The Purpose of this Book

The purpose of this book is to de-mystify the subject of selling.

There is an expression, "you can't see the forest for the trees." Selling is a lot like that.

Definitions of selling abound: Enthusiasm. Selling yourself. Being a good closer. Being a good prospector. Being persuasive. Being a good talker.

Being able to manipulate people into buying something they don't really want.

But those things are not the forest, they are all the trees. I know some very enthusiastic people who can't sell very well at all. And I know people who don't talk very well but sell like crazy.

There are dozens of books, study tapes, and seminars that deal very well with techniques and attitudes. More trees. One book on the market goes so far as to say selling cannot be defined. So the mystery continues.

I am not saying that techniques are not valuable. They are. I have studied and mastered most of them. But even after I had been selling for several years I was as mystified by a yes as I was by a no.

One problem was that no matter how many clever techniques I learned, or what my attitude was, I still got lost in the trees. Clients had a way of dreaming up more responses than the sales trainers could prepare me for.

Trees. More and more trees.

This book will describe and explain what selling is. This book will show you the complete forest.

And when you see the forest you will learn that relationship is everything. As you learn the relationships of all those techniques to one another, and their relationships to the "selling" forest, you will never be lost ag ain.

This book is for anyone who sells, whether you deal in a product, a service, or an intangible. It is for those who sell all day long as well as those who have other duties during the day besides selling. It is for supervisors, managers, shop owners, and small businesspersons.

I am happy to mention it will be especially helpful to you artists and craftsmen. I know your heart is in your work, so why not learn how to turn your work into at least enough money to pay your bills. There may be no need for you to continue to drain your creative energy waiting tables or driving taxicabs.

It is my intention that you may use this book as a reference point to help you build your selling skills. You will see as we go along that selling successfully depends on a set of skills, not on being the right or wrong personality type.

You may not need to learn how to close, or how to prospect, but you will need to learn something. This book is designed to let you know which skills are appropriate for your own individual circumstances.

If you are already selling professionally, and feel stuck, this book will show you how to get your career moving again. Or perhaps you may simply be ready to move up the selling ladder. Or perhaps you want to become a master and hit the BIG TIME. The decision is yours.

I believe selling is the most seriously underrated profession in America today. Selling offers truly unlimited opportunity for all who are willing to learn it. It is amazing how simple it is. But I don't want to mislead you. If you have big goals it will require a big effort, take a long time, and a lot of discipline. And if you want less, it will take less.

Selling doesn't care about your past. Maybe you have been just mediocre or even failed at everything else you have done. That's OK. If you are willing to put forth the effort, you will succeed.

Of all the vocations selling is the least prejudiced. You can be a man or a woman. Any race, religion, or ethnic background. Or any age. Please not that Harlan Sanders went out and started selling his famous recipe for KENTUCKY FRIED CHICKEN at the age of 65 and became a millionaire.

If you are asking the question, "But can I do it?" the answer is yes. And there is no mystery. It is a simple matter of turning your desires into skills. A far more important question to ask yourself is, "Will I do it?" So, if you are willing, let's go on an exciting adventure. An adventure in learning. An adventure in selling. And best of all, an adventure in living.

The Definition of Selling

How many times have you heard the advice, "Keep it simple?" Well for now we are going to keep it that way because the complexities will show themselves soon enough. It is very important to understand this simple definition of selling.

It is essential for you to break away from any existing stereotypes. Throw away any need to be right or wrong, or good or bad. I am not writing this book for those reasons. I am writing this book to provide understanding. Understand that when you go to a baseball game and pay one dollar for a bag of peanuts the peanut vendor has just made a sale. Please take special notice that peanut vendors don't have to be great conversationalists. They don't have to be particularly persuasive. They don't get all involved with closing, or the hard sell, or the soft sell.

They walk around with a cart full of peanuts and yell, "Peanuts, one dollar!" You hold up one finger for each bag you want, send the money down a row of your fellow baseball fans and the vendor sends you your peanuts. There has just been a sale.

It is also a sale when the Boeing Company delivers 20 jumbo jets to American Airlines for billions of dollars, or an insurance agent signs you up for life insurance. What is the simple common thread that makes all of these qualify as sales? That leads us to the definition.

To sell is to exchange. To part with for some equivalent. To give and receive reciprocally.

Professional sellers are professional exchangers. They exchange products, services, and intangibles for some equivalent. Most commonly, money.

It's the exchanging that makes it selling. That's why every seller needs a buyer. Without the reciprocity of equivalence you could have a philanthropist, who gives freely, or a thief, who takes freely.

Here are some examples of exchanges: Computers (products) are exchanged for money. Carpets are cleaned (service) for money. A radio station provides "air time"(an intangible called advertising) for money.

The exchange doesn't always have to be for money. Barter is still alive and well in America today. A farmer may exchange cheese for firewood (a product for a product). A dentist may perform dental work in exchange for carpentry work around the office (a service for a service). The IRS considers all these as sales and wants to know about them so they can be taxed.

What makes a seller a professional is the same thing that makes anyone else a professional, it is a means of livelihood. Those who don't count on that as a means of livelihood are called amateurs. There are outstanding amateur sellers just as there are outstanding amateur athletes. It takes good selling skills to earn a good livelihood, just like most other professions.

Selling is exchanging. If you keep this simple definition in mind, it will prevent you from becoming confused and overwhelmed.

A Background Profile of Selling

Let me give you a background profile of selling. It can be lots of fun. Many look at it as a game. It has basics and mechanics that, once understood, enable sellers to earn more money than any other single group of professionals in the world. More than two thirds of all upper-level management comes form the ranks of sales. We're talking here about people who run things: company owners, presidents, and vice presidents.

This is not new. 200 years ago, when America was just a baby, the dream was to expand to the west. The founding fathers recognized the need for, you guessed it, sellers. They sent out "agents" to the leading edges of the frontier to sell supplies to the pioneers, trappers, and the other adventurers who opened this nation up.

The world has changed a lot since then. So have selling techniques and working conditions. As a matter of fact, selling techniques are always changing. This is not easy to notice since so many major corporations are still using techniques that are 30 years old. All you have to do is take a walk around a few automobile dealerships to see how dreadful these old techniques can be. I find it absolutely amazing that car companies spend hundreds of millions of dollars on advertising and new car development and virtually nothing on selling techniques. It still as not dawned on these high priced executives that it is painful for us to deal with poorly trained sales personnel. How come they haven't figured out that a well-trained staff would sell not just more product, but earn goodwill too?

There is today a tremendous demand for sellers. Look at the job listings on the Internet and you will find large numbers of openings all over the country for experienced people, and many willing to take on trainees.

Titles for sales people usually get quite off the beam. Account Executive is one of the most common. (I've never been able to figure out how that came about.) Reps, or Manufacturer's Reps, are common also. Rep is short for representative. Customer Service is NOT sales, although it is common for part of the seller's job to provide customer service.

The size of the sale plays a big role in selling. Sales that are high in price are called "big ticket" items. Luxury cars, yachts, real estate and things like that.

There are several different types of selling. **Inside Sales**: When the selling is done inside a building and the customers come to you. **Outside Sales**: When the selling done outside a building and you have to go track down your customers. In the old days these were called traveling salesmen.

Telemarketing: This means you do it on the telephone. Telemarketing has grown to be so popular that customers are getting sick of it. Part of the problem is the telephone is very intimate and, therefore, very powerful. Think about that when you are using the phone. Your voice is literally right in a person's ear. In the early days there were many people who would not hang up a phone without permission. Those days are gone and now you have to get right to the point and stay on point or you will hear a quick click.

Boiler Rooms: This also means you do it on the telephone, but it also implies hard-core, high-pressure sales. Boiler Rooms are another source of very bad feelings about sellers. These people do not take no for an answer. Politeness is not acceptable. If a buyer wants to say no, he has the obligation to hang up the phone. I think these people go the Brer Bear School of Closing.

Retail Sales: This really covers a wide range of selling operations. There are small retail stores where you deliver a great deal of personal attention to the buyer. Then you have the large department stores where they train you to vanish if you see a customer who might be in need of help, or worse, actually want to buy something.

Direct Sales: This refers to those companies that skip the retail stores and sell directly to the buyer. These are companies such as Tupperware, Avon, Fuller Brush, or Amway.

Mail Order and Catalogue Sales: This is a way to sell that usually eliminates the need for direct contact with the buyer. It has been very effective for many decades and is currently developing a greater percentage of the overall market. This is a perfect way to sell if you don't have any desire to become a good talker.

Myths about Selling

Salespersons are born, not made: The truth is that selling is a skill. Anyone cable of reading this book is capable of selling. As a rule of thumb, if you can buy things you can sell things.

You must have the right personality: This is a really dopey myth. Is there a right personality for doctors? For carpenters? For gardeners? Please, give me a break. If you have the desire to sell, you have the right personality.

You have to be a good talker: To begin with, most of the good sales professionals are good listeners. I'll take a good listener over a good talker any day of the week. And, as a buyer, I am always much happier to fine a seller who listen to my problems. Also, keep in mind that talking is a skill and can be improved greatly with practice. I will tell you how to go about that in a later chapter.

You have to be a self-starter: It is true there are some sales jobs where you are completely your own boss. But, the bulk of the jobs have supervisors and task requirements just like most other jobs. Most people in most professions are not really self-starters. So, if you need structure in your work you are not alone.

You have to be highly motivated: Sure, if you want to make a ton of money. But, if you are like most people you already have the kind of motivation that is plenty for you to earn a good livelihood. Those of you who want to increase you motivation will see how to do that in the chapter on goals.

You have to be pushy: How did this get started? Sellers are just people. Some are pushy and some are not. Let me tell you that some of the highest paid professionals in the world are as gentle and as kind as you could hope for. The real problem comes from management. Most of the pressure comes from them. It is a serious and nationwide problem. I believe that if more management personnel learn what selling is really about they will decrease the insane pressure they put on the sales staff.

You have to sell on a commission: Of course this is quite common, but there are many jobs in the profession that pay a salary or wage of some kind. Often this is accompanied with a bonus or incentive plan. I personally prefer a commission basis, but it was difficult to get used to at the beginning. Many companies will begin with a salary or "draw" against commission and then convert to a commission basis after the seller as been established.

A good sales person can sell anything to anybody: To me this is the most destructive myth to the profession. It is the silliest, most idiotic idea that anyone ever came up with. This is where a lot of the mysticism about selling comes from. All of the very best sales people get told no a lot of the time. There are no exceptions. In fact, the most successful sellers get told no more often than the poor ones.

Selling is a skill. The truth is a good sales person can sell lots of things to lots of people, but through effort, not some magical ability inherited at birth.

What to Expect as You Read this Book

Before going into the approximately 50 topics to be covered, I would like to let you know what to expect as you ready this book.

This is a very complete book, so please keep a marker or pen handy. Underline ideas that interest you and make a star by the topics that require action. Also, there are numerous skills and you may want to mark them in a special way so you can be certain to add them to your repertoire. This book is also designed to make a great reference guide for long-term use.

Selling is a business of lists. Several times I will be suggesting that you get a yellow pad and write things down. Keep a yellow pad handy. Actually, it doesn't have to be a yellow pad. It can be white or beige. I don't want to be hard to get a long with.

You will find lots of dictionary style definitions. This will help keep everything on track. I will explain much of jargon of the selling profession.

These are the six basic elements of selling:

1. A product or service
2. A buyer
3. A motive or reason
4. A price
5. A decision to act (The core of the sale!)
6. A seller

It's a simple list that you will find in every sale. I will go though each element, explain it, and put in into perspective. I will give examples of what to do as well as how to do them. In the next chapter I'll go over the first five elements.

*An Introduction to Selling*

PART TWO

THE BASIC ELEMENTS

ELEMENT ONE

THE PRODUCT OR SERVICE

The first element that we are going to look at is the product or service. From a tactical standpoint it needs to be considered very early because it dramatically affects all the other elements.

It is very common to find people who have tried selling but have quit because it just isn't suitable for them. I discovered something quite interesting about these people during the dozen years I was an employment consultant, and in talking to hundreds of sellers while researching this book. Most of them were selling something they either had no interest in, or actually hated.

No wonder so many thousands of people fail in this business with a beginning like that.

In that wonderful song, When You Wish Upon A Star, it says,

> "If your heart is in your dream, no request is too extreme."

What we sell is of critical importance. Make sure that you are dealing with a product or service you can get your heart into or you are going to have a very rough time. If I had started out in this business selling insurance I know I would have

failed. Horribly. Why? Because my heart is just not into insurance. I hate insurance. I hate to buy it. But for someone who likes insurance, it can be an excellent career choice.

You are in charge of your own heart. If you cannot get behind what you sell, skip it. When I got my job as an employment consultant I really enjoyed it. I liked what I was doing and the people I was working with, so it was no surprise that I was very successful at it.

Know your product or service.

Professional singers are not any better at singing than anyone else. But you can always tell they are professionals right away because of one major difference—they don't have to hum.

Think about that.

Professional singers learn to sing at least one solid hour's worth of songs without stopping to hum. They know the words so well that even if they are temporarily distracted they don't have to ask the band to stop so they can start over at the beginning. They just go right on as if nothing ever happened.

That's how well professional sellers need to know their product or service. It makes no difference what it is. The point here is to learn it extremely well.

Sometimes it can be learned in a matter of days or weeks. Sometimes it takes years. It depends on many factors. It's a good idea to look at these factors not only to help in selecting a good product or service, but also to prepare for the necessary learning process.

Learning process? Yes. I bring this up because there are large numbers of people who are harboring some very bad notions about this. When I say "bad notions," I mean they cripple income and growth potential.

The two worst offenders are:

One, just because you graduated from high school or college, you are educated. A done deal. No more study, no more books, no more teacher's dirty looks. This is seriously incorrect.

Two, you think that just because you read something, or hear something during a training session that you have magically learned it. In reality, you have simply been introduced.

Learning about your product or service is a process. It won't happen over night, so relax. Take the time and make the effort to study, read, and digest whatever material is available to you. I guarantee that you will make extra sales on this one point alone. It's what the professionals do

A Partial, but Effective, List of Things To Know

How it works. You are supposed to know everything a buyer could want to know. You are in charge of knowledge and, in many cases, a demonstration of some kind. Stay alert and in time you will learn more from your buyers than any other single source.

How easy or difficult it is to sell. The level of difficulty is going to depend mostly on your background. But think about this. Your evaluation will have a big impact because it determines what options you will have to go about getting buyers. Know if it's simple or complex, big or small. Don't get too cocky! The penalties for miscalculating can be very severe. This is where a lot of egos get badly damaged. It is better to be on the cautions side here, because if you are wrong, it is a fairly easy to correct. Upgrading is way better than downgrading.

The quality. Just how good do you think your product or service is? Know the quality as it compares to other on the market. Know how dependable it is. If you are the sort of person who wants buyers to repeat, you had better make certain the quality is going to permit that. Does it have a guarantee?

Availability. Learn how soon it can be delivered. Learn your sources to know if you can get more, and for how long. Is it permanent? Is it seasonal? Maybe it's a night- time product or service. Where can you get it? Where can you sell it? Does it require traveling? Can you sell it from your home or do you have to work from an office or factory?

Training and education. If you need to train or educate buyers this is going to take up time. A very common mistake sellers make is not allowing for the time this can take. And this time can eat away at your profits. Allow for it.

Service. If you are obligated to perform service after the sale, and you are responsible, then this is another factor that takes time. This time can eat into your profits, so check it out very thoroughly. Keep in mind that even if you work for a company that provides support personnel to perform the service, your customer or client is going to call you when things go wrong. Angry customers can ruin an otherwise good day.

How common or unique it is. Once again, this is going to determine how you go about getting buyers. A common product or service is much more difficult because there will be a lot of competition. Getting buyers in saturated markets is a very tough job. Unique features of common items can be very helpful. For example, when black and white television sets were common, color became a very hot item. It even affected the programming. But don't kid yourself. You may think you have something unique, but if your customers have seen it before you will be clobbered with indifference.

Etcetera. Get yourself a yellow pad and begin writing down information about your product or service. Learn it well. Go through the above list as a start, but keep on adding. Keep this list handy and add to it as ideas come to you. A really good idea is to take the list to your office and ask for information from others. Memorize this information. Learn this information so well, that even if you are distracted – and buyers love to distract sellers—you can stay on track and make the sale.

How to Select a Product or Service

Begin with a yellow pad and start writing down things that interest you. Write down anything you

can think of even if it seems silly or impossible. It is very important that you write down lots of things. Make sure you have a long list whether you are new to selling or are just interested in making a career shift.

Start with the most obvious stuff. What is your favorite hobby or interest? Are you into sports? Do you like animals? What do you do in your spare time? What do you like to read about?

Keep adding to your list. Spend time and make an effort. This is one of the most important decisions you will make in your career. Take a couple of hours a week over a period of a few weeks and you will be able to come up with a great choice.

Ask family members and friends for ideas. Sometimes they see things about you that you miss. Write down some of those ideas.

Read the classified section the Sunday newspaper. You will see lots of ideas there. In fact, the entire newspaper is a good idea. You may get an idea from news items, feature stories, or advertisements.

One of my favorite stories about choosing something to sell comes from the 1984 Olympics. There was a gentleman in his mid-twenties who wanted to sell something at the Los Angeles Coliseum, but he didn't know exactly what. He didn't have a lot of money, but had some imagination.

He walked all around the place. For those of you who have never been there, let me tell you the place is huge. It was during this exploration that he saw what he could sell. Although it is more a matter of what he didn't see that provided him with his product. He didn't see very many public drinking fountains in this very large place. He knew August in Los Angels is hot.

Have you guessed by now? He sold water. By using his imagination he found a small, but quite profitable way to participate in the Olympic Games.

Water is about as obvious as you can get I like this story because it illustrates that choosing a product or service just takes a little work and imagination.

Once you have your list fairly large, begin to prioritize. Then begin to investigate your selections just as the seller checked out the Los Angeles Coliseum.

Happy dreams.

ELEMENT TWO

BUYERS

Use words like client, customer, account, purchaser, not victim, loser, opponent, or enemy.

Treat buyers with respect. Look at buyers as those who are giving you what you want. Remember the definition of selling. To exchange. You are supposed to get something of equivalence. Like money, cash, dinero.

In his book, How to Get People to Do Things, Robert Conklin says, "to the degree you give others what they want, they will give you what you want." I wrote that out on a large piece of paper and put on the wall where I could see it easily and often.

Get on their side. One of the sign of most topnotch professionals is their genuine interest in their customers. The best way to get anyone interested in you is to get interested in him or her. People who are self conscious or shy are usually thinking of themselves instead of others.

Be nice to buyers. This attitude can be cultivated and developed. Don't require them to like you. Don't argue with them. They get hassled all day long from a variety of people, so be pleasant.

Does this mean that you have to be a wimp? A doormat? No. It means you have to be tactful, graceful, compassionate, and understanding. For those of you who want to make large quantities of cash, the more of these qualities you will need. Now, I know what some of you are thinking. There are some people out there who are real jerks! Class A bozos! What about them? My advice is to take them off your list. But you don't have to be a jerk about it. Do it tactfully. This is one of the rewards of skill. There are plenty of good buyers. So why deal with those who are abusive or uncooperative?

Know Your Buyers

Know your buyers. Sounds familiar doesn't it? Everybody wants more buyers, but not everybody is willing to work for them. Some people get into retail sales because of the very false assumption that all you have to do is display your product and presto! Buyers appear like magic.

Most of these people go broke. Fast.

Large companies spend large amounts of money just studying and leaning about buyers. This is called research and development. But you don't have to have lots of money. You can do some of this on your own. If you like profits, I recommend it.

Here is a really good idea for you. Combine learning with earning. Your customers will buy from you while you learn about them. Amazing, but true. The way to do this is by using an old technique called a SURVEY. Make a note because first I'm going to go over what you want to know about buyers. Then, later,

I'm going to go over how to approach buyers, and that is where you can use this idea.

Please remember that the main purpose of this book is to de-mystify the subject of selling. When you take the time and make the effort to learn about buyers, a big chunk of the mystery will vanish.

The way to go about this is to study. This is another difficult job. You actually have to read, and re-read, and make notes as you go. Some of you, of course will enjoy this part. But, who cares? Do it whether you like it or not. I hope you appreciate this truthful approach.

Another Partial List of Things to Know

How to get them. I usually get a lot of attention when I say this. Later in this chapter I will get into some specifics, but for the moment I want to point out that this is just another skill. And since it is a skill it can be worked on. The most common methods of generating buyers are advertising and prospecting.

Where they are. They can be everywhere. At home, at work, at play. They can be at the beach, at the park, in the mountains. They can be shopping, reading, or watching television. Be wise and really start to tune in. Put the eagle eye on them. Learn their habits as well as their habitats. Begin to make lists of where you see or hear them. Be specific. Include addresses, phone numbers, or any information that will enable you to personally contact or advertise to them.

When they are around. What time during the day is best to reach them? Business people are usually at lunch from noon to one, so that is not the best time to call. Seasons play a big part. Summertime is a great time to sell snow cones at the beach. Weekends are busy time for shoppers. Of course Christmas is the biggest retail time of the year. Nighttime may be the best time to reach certain folks.

Another way to look at "time" is by events. Marriage is a unique time. Youth and maturity are very unique times. New jobs or promotions are very special times. When people are buying homes or having babies they have to buy lots of goodies.

Who they are. They can be men, women, and children. They can be students, workers, and homemakers. There are retail stores that sell clothes just to tall people or babies. Business people have special needs. Doctors, lawyers, and dentists all have special needs. But all of these folks have regular needs too. They may be rich, poor, or in between. They may be famous in some way. And don't forget whom they may know, or who may know them. Is the mystery beginning to fade? Good.

Generating Buyers

Let's talk about generating buyers. Sellers need buyers. I don't want to get too profound, but that is the ballgame. A lot of time, money, and effort are spent generating buyers. A good, competent seller can always get buyer. That does not mean you will be able to enough buyers to make a profit, but you can always get them.

An Introduction to Selling

Remember the Edsel automobile many years ago the Ford Motor Company produced? There were buyers for that. However, there were not enough buyers, so they lost a fortune.

The point I want to drive home is that if you do the work you will get buyers, even if your product or service is not so good.

In my early days as a professional I worked for a small-town radio station that had two percent of the listening audience. In radio terminology, it was called a "dog." In 90 days we tripled the billing. I can't tell you how many people told us it couldn't be done. But we did it. And I have been doing it for nearly three decades. Although I have had my Edsels, too.

There are several ways for generating buyers; advertising, promoting, coupons, contests, prospecting, and many more. I want to clear up some confusion by repeating that all of this is nothing more than generating buyers. Please don't allow yourself to get bogged down in the different methods available to you.

When I began researching this book I went to the colleges and universities and studied their course descriptions and their books. I notice they are usually listed as MARKETING AND SALES. Talk to a college student about becoming a sales person and they will cringe. They want to go into marketing.

Marketing is selling. The six basic elements exist for both. Thinking the two are somehow different causes lots and lots of confusion. For the purposes of clarity think of selling as direct, and marketing as Indirect.

Direct: refers to personal, one to one contact. Most commonly referred to as prospecting, but also know as door-to-door sales, and telephone soliciting.

Indirect: refers to ways without personal contact. Advertising, promotion, mailers, catalogues, or billboards, mail order, and word of mouth.

Indirect Methods

Indirect methods of generating buyers are very expensive, very risky, and require a fairly substantial amount of expertise. It is rare to find people who are good at these without a good deal of education and experience.

In the long run they are the most effective in terms of sheer numbers. There is no way Proctor & Gamble could reach as many buyers as they do without advertising. It's a pretty silly notion to have them hire a million telemarketers calling people at home asking them to buy some soap.

The expense involved with indirect methods makes for quite a bit of risk. Volume is the key, so if you are wrong, or even make a simple error, it can be bad news.

It is also important to understand that advertising is a skill. (Here I go again with this skill stuff.) If you plan to do it yourself you are wise to study it by reading a whole lot, and definitely take some seminars and courses at a local college. If you plan to go "big time" you will want to find out about advertising agencies. There are some geniuses out there who are worth tracking down.

The same is true for catalogue and mail order sales. I suppose those 800 and 900 telephone numbers fit close in here. When I say you are wise to study these subjects I hope you are not looking at this as some sort of punishment. This is where it really gets interesting. This where you actually learn the action steps that make things happen. Also, when you learn directly from experienced people, you will pick up on their energy. You will want to do more and more. And the more you do the more likely you are to succeed.

There are some inexpensive and free ways to use indirect methods. One way is the news release. There are thousands of trade publications, newspapers, and general interest magazines that will print a news release about your product or service for free. Free because it is not advertising, but publicity, and considered news. Go to your local library or bookstore and get a cop of the Writer's Market for the names and addresses of these publications. It even lists the kind of material they are looking for and how to approach them.

Another very effective way is public speaking. (For those of you who are good speakers.) Begin talking to service organizations, clubs, or any group that needs speakers. This takes a lot of effort but can pay off in a big way.

Write yourself a one-page description of your topic and background to use when you begin contacting these organizations. And keep track of them because many times they book speakers months in advance and you will want to make sure you present your material to them when they are ready. Also, let them know you are available in case they have a cancellation.

There is a hamburger stand in my neighborhood that has been really busy with customers for 25 years. Lots of places have really good food and don't do this kind of volume, so I used to wonder where all these people came from. Then one day I was sitting at a booth and saw the answer. On the wall were several photographs of baseball teams he had been sponsoring for years. All over the area where the kids played baseball was the name of his hamburger stand on the t-shirts the kids were wearing. Not only does he build his business, but by sponsoring the teams he makes a contribution to the community and develops

intense loyalty.

Finally, just use some imagination. You will be delighted and surprised at your ability to come up with some way of generating buyers that will work

Direct Methods

The most common name for the direct method is *prospecting*. It is one of the most difficult tasks you will be faced with. There is no advantage in sparing the truth about this subject since no one escapes it. It is plain, hard work. So as you approach this subject, brace yourself.

Prospecting is what determines your income.

This is where you decide, with great accuracy, how much money you will earn in any calendar year. Through prospecting you can determine with 10 or 20 percent how much money you will make. Sound like a good deal? That means that if you become skilled at prospecting and you set a goal to earn $50,0000 in one year, you can safely predict that at the end of the year your income will be between $40,000 and $60,000.

That also means that if you are at a plateau in your income right now, or if you hit a plateau later, you can devise an effective plan to increase your income by a specific amount.

All the other skills are factors, but it is prospecting, and prospecting alone, that determines the amount of money you make.

Prospecting is a critical skill. Don't let this one slide. It is the foundation of your work. If you are weak at everything else, and only strong in this one area, you will be able to predict your income. This is where you make it happen. This is where you pace yourself to go fast or slow, hard or easy.

Just to make the deal even better, after you have worked very hard on your prospecting for a certain period of time it ultimately becomes easy. Easy in the same way that a professional baseball player catches those routine fly balls hit to the outfield. They make it look easy. By the time we see them it is easy. What we don't see are the years of hard work it took to get there.

Prospecting for buyers is just like prospecting for gold, in that you are looking for something of value. It is simply a matter of talking to people. And, as J. Douglas Edwards says on his cassette recording, P's & Q's, Prospecting & Qualifying, "the more people you see, the more sales you will make. Period."

How? To begin you need to recognize that lists are basic to prospecting. In order to make lot of contacts, whether in person or on the phone, you must have very thorough lists. Right of the bat, this very hard work. It takes a lot of detail work, searching, writing, and filing. You can purchase lists but they are costly and still lots of work.

Much of my experience in prospecting has been on the telephone. If I have a solid, well-prepared list in front of me, I can make 100 plus calls a day. I don't like to make that many calls, but I can. The type of product or service you are dealing with will determine the amount of contacts you should make daily. It is your job to determine what this number is, and to see to it that the contacts are made. Again I say, don't let this slide. So many times sales people get all wrapped up in making deals and skip the prospecting calls. Then, a month or two later they get depressed and all bent out of shape because the sales fall off.

If you are selling something that you are only selling once, you won't be able to go as fast, but you still may need a thorough, comprehensive list.

Your lists need to be organized in some fashion in order to hit peak effectiveness. A file box with 3 by 5 cards is one of the most popular ways of keeping lists organized. There are some computer software packages that are good, too. Talk to fellow sellers, and make visits to well-stocked office supply stores for ideas that suit your own particular needs.

A Few Methods of Prospecting.

The dreaded cold calling method.

This is a very, very, effective way to get buyers. It simply means that after you have compiled your list you start contacting people "cold." In other words, perfect strangers. And this is a good time to bring up another major reason why this is difficult—rejection! Lots and lots of rejection! You really are better off knowing that it is facing you. (In a later chapter I will give you a simple, two-step method for dealing with it, but for now it is just important to know that it is there.) Volume is the key to cold calling, whether it is in person or on the phone. Follow-up is also very important, so you need to maintain some level of organization.

This method has tremendous advantages for anyone who is new to a specific market. I hope this makes sense. When you are new and don't know anyone there are very few methods available. This offers you a chance to build a client base.

A special philosophical note: When you are cold calling, you need to make a decision about whom you are going to talk to. For those of you without experience you will be surprised to learn that you can get some people talking for a long time without getting down to a decision. Some people love to just chat, especially if they are bored, or if you are just fun to talk to. Here is the crux of your decision to hang up or keep probing: is the prospect interested in your product or service already, or should you keep talking and try to build interest? It is up to you to decide and is matter of personal taste. I move on extremely fast if they are not interested in my opening statement. I feel I am much more productive if I spend my time making additional calls to locate someone who is already interested in what I have to sell. There is no right or wrong here, there is only what makes you comfortable and productive.

Referral prospecting.
To me this is ideal if you are dealing with a big ticket or medium size product or service. It is so much easier and effective to call someone and say you were referred by someone they know. This method takes a little time to kick in, but you can reach a point where you have more business than you can handle. I know, because I have done this. And it is wonderful. Basically you just learn to ask everyone you deal with, "who do you know?"

This is commonly called networking. Begin attending business mixers, expos, conventions, luncheons, breakfasts, or any gathering of people with similar interests. If you can do it without being a pest, ask friends, neighbors, or relatives for names. Some people will be glad to help, while others will act as if you have just stuck them with a safety pin.

A great source of names is a customer who has just bought from you. An excellent technique is to take five 3 by 5 cards and place them in front of you and ask them if they can think of anyone. Limit yourself to five for the time being so you don't overwhelm your customer. Remember that when you ask someone whom they know, you are asking them to recall the whole world and they may go blank. Break it down into smaller groups by saying something like, "Is there anyone at your place of work? Or, do you go to church? Or, do you belong to any clubs?"

Survey method.
This is a great way to get business and to research buyers at the same time. It is very simple. Write down information that you want to know about your potential customers. Create questions from this. Do you use so & so type products? How many of this and that do you use in a month? What company are you now using for "blank" at this time? If you ask intelligent questions, you will be surprised at how much information people will give you. The really neat part is that some of these people will actually become buyers. This method takes some serious work and planning. Keep in mind that people are busy and they will hang up on you, or slam the door in your face if you ask stupid, pointless question.

I have just touched upon three methods of prospecting. There are many more available to you. This is such an important part of selling that I want to encourage you to go the library or bookstore and learn all you can about them. This makes a big difference in your success.

How to approach buyers.

Studies indicate that the average American receives more than 2000 messages a day to buy things. This includes radio and television ads, billboards, magazines, newspapers, wives, children, and everything. So it is not a surprise to find some resistance when you or I just happen to call with yet another request.

Once you reach someone, either on the phone or in person, you have about 20 to 30 seconds before they decide to let you go on, or reject you. So you had better make those seconds count.

Write out a script. That is how it's done. Do not wing it. This part is fairly easy. There are two things everyone wants to know when anyone calls them. Who you are, and why you are calling. I always begin my script by saying, "Hello, my name is Larry Yslas with the XYZ Company and the reason I am calling is..."

All you have to do is write out 20 to 30 seconds worth of reasons.

Here are a couple of short examples.

"I have a new gadget that will save you 50 percent on your monthly fuel bill without interrupting your present system, are you interested in something like that?"

"My company has a service that provides more effective delivery for your products and we will pick up at your door, saving you time and effort, does that sound like something you could use?

After you have written out a script, Practice it so that is sounds natural. Try it out and see how it goes. Talk to others who are in your office and learn what they say. If possible, have group sessions where you can work on script together. When they don't work out, either change them or throw them out and star over from scratch. But you will find something that works effectively.

One final note on all of this. Even the best scripts become old over time because our prospects begin to recognize them and build up resistance. So, periodically re-work your material in some way to keep it, and you, fresh and interesting.

Qualifying buyers.

We always hear a lot about buyers rejecting sellers, but sellers have to learn how to reject buyers, too. The amount of time and effort wasted on *unqualified* buyers is staggering. I have seen poorly trained sales people waste hours talking to prospects that never had any intention or ability to buy their product or service.

This is another critical function for anyone interested in increasing his or her income. Learn this. Become good at it.

What this all means is that you can, and should, determine immediately if the person you are talking to has the intention and the ability to buy. The way you do this is to question and observe.

When you approach people state what it is that you have to sell. If the prospect expresses interest begin to question that interest. This may take anywhere from a few seconds to a few hours, depending on your product or service. It is very simple to do.

Let's start by looking at the most common of all qualifying problems, money. As soon as you are satisfied that interest has been expressed and you have briefly stated what you have to sell, you now say to your prospect, "If I can deliver my product or service, it will cost exactly this many dollars, can your budget handle that?"

There are other ways of doing this, but don't kid yourself, this is usually the best way. Don't spend time going through a detailed demonstration without the knowledge that there could be a paid sale. The problems that come up by stating price early are tiny and easily solved. The problems that come by waiting too long are huge, horrible, time consuming, hard to solve, cause bad feelings, and sometimes wind up in court.

If you are afraid that price is going to chase buyers away, you have a serious problem. Talk to you supervisor or someone with experience if you feel this way. Get comfortable about how much things cost. I am proud to charge money. I work hard, I am honest, and when I cash my check I feel that both my client and me have benefited.

The next types of questions you want to ask are basic information questions. In order to effectively provide a product or service you need to know things about the buyer. The more details you have the better

An Introduction to Selling

off you are. It's yellow pad time again. The only way to know details is to start writing them down.

For example, if you are selling cars you want to know how the buyer is planning on using the car. If the buyer is a homemaker with three kids in school and wants a car for basic transportation, you will sell a car that fits those needs. If the buyer is a single executive and wants a car for fun, you will sell a car that fits those needs.

The point here is to ask sufficient questions so you have a thorough and intelligent understanding of the needs and wants of your prospect so you can make a presentation that is going to be hard to resist.

This is a tough issue. Spend some time on it. Another thing that will happen by making the effort to qualify your buyers is that you can figure out what motivates them. Everyone has a motive. It is the next element of selling I am going to cover.

ELEMENT THREE

MOTIVES

A motive is a reason.

Please dwell on that. It is a common goal of sales people and managers to be good motivators. We want to motivate our customers to buy. Managers want to motivate sales people to work hard.

I love detective stories and one of my favorite detectives is Columbo. He always has a murder mystery to solve. The most important thing he always wants to know is the motive. This is true for real-life detectives, too. Why would someone want to murder the victim? Once a motive is established, the case is close to being solved.

Why would anyone want to buy your product or service? When you know the answer to that, you gong to make a lot of sales. Providing, of course, you do your prospecting.

Motives can be based on logic or they can be based on emotion. It is because they can be based on emotion that this subject can make you crazy. In case you haven't been around human beings very long, I would like to inform you that we are nuts. Wacko. There are times when every one of us ought to be kept in a little, padded room.

Is it any wonder? No matter where you live on this planet, no matter who you are, no matter your age, no matter your social position, you can be instantly subjected to earthquakes, tornadoes floods, fires, hurricanes, or volcanic eruptions. Add to that, invading armies, robbers, terrorists, and the Internal Revenue Service. Try not to take this stuff too seriously.

Emotions can be extremely powerful motivating forces. So powerful that even the most inept seller cannot stop a buyer who is moved emotionally to buy.

What I want to do most with this subject is shed light on it, because this is not a skill. You can learn to recognize motives, but each one of us does things for our own reasons. I became much better as a seller when I started concentrating on my client's reasons and stopped giving them mine.

In my early months as an employment consultant I would call up applicants and tell them about these absolutely terrific jobs. Terrific for all of my reasons. I experienced lots of rejection, canceled interviews, no-shows, and turndowns of offers from employers. I didn't like that at all. It was a serious waste of my time.

Then I learned one of the great lessons of successful selling. My clients didn't care about my reasons. And, I will confess, it was a blow to my ego. They cared about their reasons. That is the real secret to being a good motivator. So, obviously, the trick is to be able to determine what they are.

Probably the best way to do this is to ask. This whole thing starts to get very complicated because sometimes they don't know. Sometimes they don't care. Sometimes they know, but won't tell you. Sometimes they know what sellers are up to. They may feel that if you figure out what their true motive is, they will be at a disadvantage. Pretty wild, isn't it?

A popular term for the true desire of a buyer is the Hot Button. Once you do know the buyer's hot button it is very important to push it every time you talk to the buyer. Another very important thing to remember is to skip all other reasons. A few years ago I purchased a photocopier for my office because i go tiered of having to run down the street to the printer. My hot button was convenience, but the sales rep kept on talking about all the tax advantages. I had to tell her twice that I didn't care about that. She was wasting her time and mine.

Some common buying motives are pride, profit, security & protection, satisfaction of emotion, comfort & convenience, and fear. Fortunately, you don't always have to know what the motive is to make a sale. That sales girl who sold me the copier never did figure it out. But, overall, she did a very good job and earned her commission.

Sometimes the best you can do is just test them. Try one motive out and see what happens. Profit motivation is very popular and works quite well. Offer the prospect a reduction in price and see if they go for that. But a word of caution on offering discounts. If you do it too early in your negotiating and you are wrong, you will still have to give the discount when you finally discover the real hot button. That is money out of your pocket.

Another excellent motivator is what sellers like to call an impending event. That is where you tell the prospect that if they don't decide right now, they will lose out in some way. If you are a real estate agent, and you have a prospective buyer for a house who wants to wait before making a decision, an impending event could be the owners have just learned they have to leave the country for six months and if they can't find a buyer with 24 hours they are taking their house off the market until they return. Another impending event is a price increase. Buy now or you will have to pay more later on. We have all heard these before. Half the time they are big fat stories. But sometimes they are true.

The best method of all is learning how to interview people properly in the very beginning. Learn to ask open-ended questions. I still use a technique I learned when I was a newspaper reporter many years ago. I always write out the question words, who?, what?, when?, where?, why?, how? I systematically go through and ask as many questions as I can think of that start with these words. It works like a charm. Try it.

After you have established what you feel the hot button is, repeat it and get an agreement from you buyer. Say something like, "As I understand it, you want such and such, for such and such reasons." Repeat it exactly as they said it to you. STOP. Do not continue until they agree by saying, "Yes, that is just what I want." For small, inexpensive products or services this may take only 60 seconds. For major, complex, and expensive products or services, this can take hours. But, in the long run, it saves a lot of time and increases your effectiveness

People buy things for their reasons. Keep your efforts on that, and I promise you will make sales.

ELEMENT FOUR

PRICE

Price is the balance of every sale. The best price is when both the seller and the buyer feel like winners.

Many times a buyer will want to buy a product or service but just doesn't feel it is worth it. At that point the seller can lower the price, throw in something extra, or go find another buyer.

Price can be a very emotional issue. Some people have serous hang-ups about money. Some people hate it when someone else makes a profit. Some sellers think they should raise their prices every five minutes.

But most buyers are interested in value. And I believe that most sellers are interested in fairness. When you study the history of successful businesses you will find value and fairness are hallmarks. Remember that all sellers are also buyers. Make value and fairness your hallmark and you, too, will win.

Earlier I wrote about how it is usually a good idea to bring up price early. Many decades ago there was a gentleman by the name of James Cash Penney. He wanted to bring a bold, new idea to retail pricing. And that idea was to have one price only! That price would be marked on each item and it would not be subject to negotiation. Well, not only do we still have J.C. Penney's department stores, most retail stores use that pricing method to this very day.

An Introduction to Selling

When in doubt, be open and up front abut your prices. Experience will teach you any variations that you need to learn. Remember, it can be a pleasure to pay out money. I know that when I have lots of money and I am able to pay for the products and services that I want or need, I'm very happy about it.

ELEMENT FIVE

DECISIONS – THE CORE OF THE SALE

Commitment to action. "Yes, I will buy this and give you money."

This is when a prospect actually becomes a buyer. This is the core of the sale. This is what sellers plan for and work for. This is when we "ring the bell." This is when we get to celebrate.

So why is this part so difficult? Why is it that getting decisions is even more difficult for most sales people to learn than prospecting? Well, I'm going to tell you why. Then, I'm going to tell you how to get decisions. And furthermore, I'm gong to make it easy.

Why Getting Decisions is Difficult

Americans are not trained how to make decisions. Consequently, most aren't very good at it. Everyone is constantly telling us what to decide, but how to actually go through the process is rarely discussed. It is much too large of a subject for me to completely get into here, but I will cover enough to get you started.

Some people are so bad at making decisions they even agonize over choosing a movie on Saturday night. Seriously. You must know people like that. They are afraid they are going to make a bad decision. The thing to learn about making decisions is that everyone makes some bad decisions. Far too many of us are overly concerned with being right. And, as my friend says, "there are a lot more interesting things to be, than right.

Trained decision makers learn to make decisions quickly, and then change their minds only after they have had the opportunity to see those decisions completely through. But what most people do is start worrying that it is a bad decision even before they make it.

Decision Making is a Process

Everyone has their own decision making process. Good or bad, it is their process. The job of the successful seller is to learn it, not judge it. When you argue with buyer, not only do you lose a lot of battles, you lose a lot of time, money, and effort.

Learn to observe the decision making process so that when a buyer has actually made a decision, you'll know when to stop. Some people make decisions while they are in an emotional state. They need to be prepared to make some decisions.

Don't be confused here, because buyers usually make decisions without the help of the seller. This is especially true for small, everyday items, but also for major products or services. Experience will teach you when to know the difference.

Think of preparing buyers for decisions just like preparing to cook a delicious roast. First you need to add seasoning: A little of this, and a little of that, in just the right amounts. Too much, or too little, can spoil it.

But then it needs time to cook. If you don't allow enough time, or if you leave it in too long, it comes out tough and hard to chew.

Buyers need the proper amount of information. Too little, or too much can spoil the decision. Also, they need the right amount of time for the information to soak in and for their decision-making standards to take hold.

Another thing that is very important to learn is to set the stage. Let's go back to our delicious roast. If you are serving that roast and all you want to do is feed someone and send them on their way, paper plates and plastic cups in front of a television set will do the job. But what if you want to impress someone and make him or her feel special? You set the stage. First, you may serve some wine. Play some nice music. Of course you bring out the best china and silverware. Maybe some candles, depending on what kind of impression you are trying to make.

See the difference? Don't expect to get a big, important decision from a client with a poorly executed presentation. Make sure you client is in a place where there are no interruptions. Instead of a busy office, arrange for a conference room or a quiet restaurant. Have all of you material completely ready. Dress properly for the occasion. Make an effort here and you will get good results.

How to Get Decisions

In professional selling this is most commonly referred to as closing. This may come as a shock to some of you, but closing is not a critical skill. Prospecting is critical. I know lots of well-paid professional sales people who never, or rarely, close. They simply allow the buyers to volunteer their decisions. And about 80% of the time, I do exactly the same thing.

So if it isn't critical, why learn to do it? Here are three good reasons. One, it's worth 20% more money each year. My reward for leaning how to close is that I make about 20% more sales than the seller who has not taken this option. Two, it is a real booster for self-confidence. The is a great feeling that comes along with knowing what to do when some says, "I want to think it over," or, "Maybe." Three, it is easy to learn and easy to do. It only takes about 50 to 75 hours worth of study and training over a one or two year period of time. That breaks down to about 30 minutes a week. Now if that isn't worth a 20% lifetime pay hike, skip it.

Closing

Let's begin with what closing is. Closing is leading the buyer to a decision. Any decision. It is very important to understand that it is not making the buyer say yes.

It is indecision that drives most sellers crazy. We all get noes and we all get yeses no matter how good or bad we are. It is the indecision that kills us. Of course we are looking for a yes. But if that is our only aim, the buyer senses this and builds up resistance. But when the task simply is to get any decision, much more progress can be made

Please think about this. I make it very easy for my clients to tell me no. Isn't that a shocker? But, they open up to me. They can sense that I am not there to do battle with them. It just so happens that sometimes they should tell me no. It is dopey to think that no matter what they say there is some perfect response to get them to say yes.

By getting a no in an easy and sincere way, you have the best opportunity to discover why. The buyer trusts you. You'll feel better, too, because you now have something to deal with. Indecision is a very tough thing to handle. But worse than indecision, is a closed attitude. Upon hearing the true reason for the no, you may agree, or you may disagree with the buyer, but are in position to show your idea in a better light.

Your job as a seller is not to get people to say yes or no, you job is to help people to decide. That's what closing is.

Special note for those of you who have a large percentage of prospects who are indecisive, more than 30 percent, you have a problem with your qualifying skills. Properly qualified buyers are most often going to buy without any closing effort on the seller's part. So, you will need to make a special effort on that as well as learning closing skills. You will find that the two skills are very closely related and fairly easy to learn. Not learning them is much more difficult

To become an effective closer it is important to keep it in perspective. It takes most people at least a couple of yes to get good at it. You don't need to use closing techniques on every sale, but you need to be prepared to close on every sale.

One question that always comes up from sellers is when to close. The time to close is when you want a decision form the buyer. This is a judgment call, so naturally you will do better with experience. But basically, after you have qualified your buyer, presented your product or service, and discussed price, is when you want to close. Don't make this too complicated.

One of the reasons why closing is so easy is that you can do it more than one time. It's wonderful. Whenever you attempt a close and fail, you can do it again. And again. Studies indicate that the more you try, the more likely you are to succeed.

Closing has little to do with pressure. Everyone has heard about high-pressure sellers. Well, guess what? The real problem is with high-pressure buyers. These are folks who love to give sales people a hard time. Really. They believe they are supposed to throw up every objection they can think of. They believe it is un-American to accept a price without negotiating. They think they are supposed to "test" the integrity of the seller. As a skilled and experienced seller, I can deal with most of these types very well. But some of them are a major pain in the neck and are not worth it. Do not deal with them if you are being deprived of prospecting time. Pay close attention to what I just said. You know how long it takes you to prospect for a new buyer. "Measure the closing time against the prospecting time, and when it takes longer to close than to prospect, stop.

Forget about all this pressure business. Apply as much pressure as you feel like. You are in charge of your own pressure gauge. Your personality and style determine this. If someone is pressuring you to pressure your clients, sit down with them and discuss it. Reduce this to problem of human relationships, not selling skills.

The Dreaded Topic of Objections

Before going over some actual closes, it is necessary to discuss objections. People have objections when they want to buy, not when they don't want to buy. Let that sink in. People have objections when they want to buy. If you are having trouble with this, write that sentence on a card and place it where you can see it every day. Experienced sales people hear music when they hear an objection.

Don't take a combative attitude toward objections. They are not something designed to prevent you from making a sale. They represent an opportunity for you to increase your knowledge of the buyer, and are more likely to lead to a sale than not.

There are four basic times when you can deal width objections.

1. When they occur. This is when rookies like to answer them. This is when some buyers can really run sellers ragged. Some sellers are so good at this they can answer dozens of objections with very creative rebuttals. It's sort of entertaining. Old=fashions sales people are real big on this also. During the 1950's and 1960's buyers were less sophisticated and could be easily manipulated. Today, even if you do answer all of those objections, they find it quite easy to tell you no or to simply stall. As a rule of thumb, answer the objection as it occurs, only if the timing is correct.

2. Later. If you are in the process of qualifying, or in the middle of a presentation, and the buyer brings up an inappropriate objection, all you do is say, "I'm glad you brought that up and I will be covering that just a little later." Then continue with your work. You are in charge here. It is your job to see to it that you stay on track. Remember that some of these objections are only friendly comments. The buyer just wants to participate in the conversation. Some other good phrases to learn: "Stay with me," "Don't go wandering off, I'll get to that point," "Slow down, you're way ahead of me." Write these phrases on cards and learn them.

3. Before they occur. You are going to hear most objections over and over again. If you are hearing certain objections a whole lot, then you want to start bringing them up before the buyer does. You can turn a negative into a positive, and save a lot of time and effort by doing this. Let's say your product or service is unusually high in price. 'By bringing the subject up early you can soften the blow. You can break the price down into smaller parts, or stress small monthly payments, or discuss why the price is so high. Perhaps your product or service has a flaw of some kind. You can actually use this as an approach by bringing up the flaw first, and then talk about the good points.

4. Never. That's correct. You don't need to answer every objection. As buyers we are not usually 100 percent happy width every single thing we buy. So relax. If you have told the buyer you would cover a certain objection later, and you both forget, that's great. This happens a lot, if you let it. Automatically, if it is truly important to the buyer, it will be brought up again.

The way to become good at dealing with objections is to memorize the rebuttals. All of them. This is so easy that it is inexcusable not to do so. This is not a big job. Take a yellow pad and write down all the common objections. Then write down the rebuttals. Then memorize them. Take a few minutes a day until you have them all memorized. In most cases it will only take about 20 to 30 total hours. If you livelihood depends on this, how can you not do it? If you work with other sales people, this can be an excellent group activity.

Some Closing Techniques

Now that you are ready to get decision, here are some techniques for you to use. These techniques have been around for a long time and work quite well. One thing that is necessary to learn about asking any closing question is that you have to stop talking and wait for a response. This is important because if you utter a single word, you'll blow it. Sometimes it may even take a few minutes. This silence will take a while to get used too, but it isn't difficult.

THE BASIC CLOSE

This is also called the order blank close because you ask for information from your order form. This is a very common and very effective close. Ask a question from the top of the form. "How do you spell your last name?" or, "What is your correct mailing address?"

Then you continue asking questions until you have completed your form. This is an assumptive close. That means you assume they are going to buy, and let them stop you if they are not. We have all been sold things with this method.

THE ALTERNATE OF CHOICE CLOSE

In this close you give the buyer a choice of two decisions: "Which do you prefer, the red or the blue?" "Will that be cash or charge?" "Will you pick it up now, or would you like it delivered?"

That's pretty simple, isn't it? (I told you closing was easy,) You can also do this with three or four choices.

THE BEN FRANKLIN CLOSE

When Benjamin Franklin had a decision to make, he would draw a line down the middle of a piece of paper and write "reasons for" and "reasons against" on opposite sides. Then he would total each side to see which had the greatest total. I'm sure you have seen this done before. As a closing device it is very effective. If you have customers who are having a difficult time making up their minds, get out a yellow pad and tell them the story of Benjamin Franklin.

THE NEGATIVE-POSITIVE CLOSE

This is one of my favorite ways to close. It is set up so that a no means yes. I was watching a James Bond movie once and he used this technique to make a date with a beautiful woman. It goes like this: "Can you think of any reason why we shouldn't have dinner tonight?" "Can you think of any reason why you wouldn't want to complete this order for 500 bolts?"

This close is good because if they say yes, you can ask about it. If they say no, you have a deal. One real estate agent used it this way, right after prospects had looked at his house, "Why don't you buy it?"

This close takes a little getting used to.

PUPPY DOG OR SAMPLE CLOSING

The best way to get someone to take a puppy is to let him or her have it overnight. They will fall in love with the little critter. You know how that goes.

Many years ago I sold soap door-to-door. It was one of those concentrated products that you had to mix yourself. I walked around my neighborhood and gave a sample that was already mixed to several homes. There was an instruction sheet and a notice that I would call back n a week. It was a very good cleaner and I sold quite a lot using this technique.

Do you have a product or service that could be left overnight?

There are dozens of closes. It is a serious misconception to think that one terribly clever question or phrase is going to do the job. I have heard that enthusiasm is the key to closing. I'd like to strangle the person who inflicted that notion on the American public. Closing is a skill. Enthusiasm is a state of mind. Now I am going to teach you how to become a skilled and effective closer, without fail.

The Steps to Effective Closing

1. Make a commitment that you are going to do this. How can you expect to get decisions if you can't make them? This is a 50 to 75 hour job that will take about one to two years. (What else have you got to do?) It is also going to cost you some money, so budget for it.
2. Learn the words that mean yes. Those are yes, certainly, sure, and, absolutely. These words do not mean yes, probably, I think so, I hope so. There is no sense in fooling yourself about this. When you hear the words that don't mean yes you must stop and ask for clarification. Just say something like, "excuse me, but when say, "probably," does that mean yes? That's all there is to it. But it is critical, and you can't let it slide.
3. Study. You will need to attend a couple of seminars or workshops, read a couple books, listen to some

recordings, and read a few magazine articles. If you work with other sellers, or know others, talk to them. The point here is get a solid understanding of what closing is all about. How To Master The Art Of Selling, by Tom Hopkins is a great book to get you started.
4. Memorize and rehearse 20 closes. Get some 3 by 5 cards and spend a few minutes each day gong over these closes. As you read and study, write down the closes on the 3 by 5 cards. It is important to rehearse these closes Look at them as word tools. What will happen is this: as you become familiar with closing, and memorize even the first few, you will automatically find yourself using them. Because you have paid the price of study and rehearsal, you will discover how easy this is. You may want to memorize more than 20 closes and get really good, but 20 will make you money.
5. Practice. The first few times you try these closing techniques you may not be so good at them. But, with practice, you will improve. There is absolutely nothing mysterious or chancy about this skill.

Buyer's Remorse.

Sometimes buyers change their minds, and cancel sales. I hate it when that happens. We all do. But it is part of the business, so you may as well accept it. If you sell something small in price, an occasional cancellation is no problem. However, if you lose a deal worth thousands of dollars, a cancellation can be real depressing. It can ruin a whole day. So what do you do about?

Don't panic. When you first hear about a cancellation, remain calm and go gather information. Why is the buyer canceling? Pretend you are qualifying for the first time. Pretend this is a new sale. Hear what the buyer has to say. Then, if possible, get a new decision. By taking this approach you will be able to save some cancellations.

An ounce of prevention is worth a pound of cure. The best way to prevent cancellations is to cement the sale at the time you make it. There are several things you can do besides taking the money and running

Thank the buyer for doing business with you.

Ask for a referral. What buyer is going to cancel after giving you names of friends or associates?

Tell the buyer about any guarantees or warranties. Explain any special conditions that may come up.

Clearly discuss what is going to happen about billing, delivery, or any follow-up that is necessary. Give dates or times.

Push the buyer's hot button one last time. Congratulate the buyer for making such a good decision.

Make sure you leave your telephone number and instructions about how to reach you or your company in case questions arise. Please remember that it is normal for buyers to feel some regret about these decisions. Their friends and relatives can do a real job on them after you have gone away, so you are better off encouraging the buyer to contact you

Finally, if you are having for than 10 percent cancellations, you are probably not doing a good job of qualifying or closing. You will have to take a close look at your work and see where the problem is.

SPECIAL CONSIDERATIONS

Skills

The dictionary defines skill as a craft or trade. One of the major problems that I have seen in my many years of professional selling is the notion that selling is something over witch you have little, or no, control. This is because it has not been seen as a skill. Of course, the cat is now out of the bag. Selling is a skill. And if you practice and train, you will improve.

About 10 percent of you will want to make huge amounts of money. However, most of you will just want to earn a good income. Most of you will not want to put in the tremendous amount of effort required to make a lot of money.

During the Olympic games in Munich 19j76, Mark Spitz won 7 gold medals. He also won 2 gold medals during the previous games in Mexico. Of course, he was born with certain abilities. But did you know that he started to swim at the age of seven? And did you know that by the time he won those medals he had spent 14,000 hours in a swimming pool? (I'm surprised he didn't look like a prune.) Based on a 40-hour workweek, 50 weeks a year, we work 2000 hours a year. So, Mark did not rely only upon natural talent. He practiced and trained 14,000 hours.

Barbra Streisand became on overnight sensation at the age of 18. Did you know she started singing seriously at the age of three? Fernando Valenzuela became a star pitcher for the Los Angeles Dodgers at the age of 19. He started pitching actively at age eight. He was pitching in semi-pro baseball games at the age of twelve.

Benny Goodman was one of the most talented and famous musicians in the world. Many years ago Frank Sinatra used to tour with him. Sinatra noticed that during off-hours Goodman was always practicing with his clarinet. He once commented, "How come you are always practicing with that clarinet? You don't need to practice to be good." Goodman replied, "You are right. I am good if I don't practice. But I'm not great!

The Big 10 Percent

It takes effort to improve skills. Benjamin Franklin says in his autobiography, "No pain, no gain." That was 200 years ago, and he wasn't talking about weightlifting. If you are going to make gains in anything, from your income, to your skill, you are gong to have to work at it.

Whether you have lots of talent, or little talent, practice and training will make you skills better. My suggestion is to dedicate 10 percent of your work time to this. If you work 40 hours a week, that means you could be spending 4 hours on practice and training.

This is about 40 minutes a day. Even if you only spend 15 minutes a day, you will become better than most professionals in business today.

By spending the energy on training and practice you will also discover that you will enjoy your job more. Some of you may be under the false assumption that jobs are fun. Or not fun. That is a juvenile point of view. Jobs are what you make them. Make your job really great. It's up to you. If you are in a situation that is bad, then improve your skills so you will qualify for a better one.

Develop the proper habits. Read daily. Listen frequently to recordings. Attend seminars. I like to attend three or four seminars a year. Seminars can be lots of fun. They last anywhere from one hour to two weeks. If you can, travel to another city to take a major seminar. It becomes stimulating as well as informative. Stay in a nice hotel. Treat yourself as if you were a very special person. You deserve it, because you are a very special person. Another great thing about seminars is that you get to be around other people in the field. You may make a friend.

Time & Timing

Most really good things take time. Thomas Edison had to try 10,000 times before he could make a light bulb work. Can you imagine how he felt when he failed on attempt number 5,456? Do you think he got depressed? Or discouraged? I can hear his friends and relatives, "Thomas, Thomas, Thomas, (people always say you name three times whenever they are going to tell you something for your own good) be realistic! Get a job you can depend on. You can't make light come from a hunk of glass. People are starting to talk."

It took awhile, but today we have light bulbs. I sure like them. And, as soon as he completed his invention, he started selling like crazy. It may take you some time to achieve your goals. It may take time to develop a special account. It may take time to build a sales rote. So maybe last week, or last year, was a disaster. Just stop and think how Edison felt after attempt number 5,456, and keep going.

Timing is also something to consider. You have all heard of the ticker tape. It's that tape with the little holes that carry lots of information so popular on stock exchanges. Well, our friend Thomas Edison invented that, too. Only his timing on that was not so hot. There was no one around to use it at that time. He vowed he would never again invent anything for which there were no available buyers.

Ask yourself if the timing is good for your product or service. Make sure the timing is good for the skill you want to develop. Maybe it's better timing to learn how to close before you start building up a new territory. May it's better timing to lean more effective advertising techniques before you take on management responsibilities.

Think about time and timing. Don't sit around waiting for things to happen to you. Use your imagination. Take some risks. I guarantee you are going to mess up some of the time. But I also guarantee you will do really terrific some of the time, too.

Fears

Selling is a profession that absolutely forces us to deal with fears. We all have them in a big way. If you are in your twenties you may deny this, but those of you who are older know better. Franklin Roosevelt once said, "We have nothing to fear, but fear itself." It is still true. That is why it is so important to take a look at it. I am not an expert on this subject at all. It has been one of the biggest problems in my life. And, as near as I can tell, it is a life-long issue.

Fear is insidious. It hides inside of us and camouflages itself so that we have difficulty shining light on it. When we are children we are usually afraid of the dark. We call to our parents during the night when we think we see something that scares us. Our parents come into the room and turn on the light (the one invented by Thomas Edison) and the fear goes away. I hope to shed a little light on the subject so some it will go away. As professional sellers, we are faced with fear not only in ourselves, but also in our buyers

Fear of rejection is such a common fear that many people are forced to give up selling as a career. It can be overcome, however, with this simple two-step process:

First, it needs to be dealt with on a psychological level. It is not you, personally, that is being rejected.

An Introduction to Selling

Remember, when prospecting to strangers, you are one of two thousand requests that person is receiving daily. He or she is turning down your product or service. If you still feel it is you, then go to work on your personality. In the next two parts of this book are many things you can work on to improve yourself.

Second, go out and be rejected a few hundred times After you have been rejected that often you will become so well conditioned you will no longer consider it a problem. Or at least you may stop throwing up.

Finally, if you make no progress on your own, talk to a psychologist. They have a great track record in solving this type of problem, normally with very few visits.

PART THREE

TOOLS OF THE TRADE

"If the only tool you have is a hammer,
you tend to see every problem as a nail"
…Abraham Maslow

An Introduction to Selling

Organization

Organization is another one of those very difficult tasks that has to be dealt with by most people who choose selling as a career. The resistance to this subject is nothing short of phenomenal. However, the rewards are also phenomenal.

This is a power tool. Some dictionary definitions are; to give structure, to systematize, to start. Everyone needs some organization. Selling is a business of lists. Lists of customers, leads, inventory, objections, rebuttals, closes, meetings, goals, activities, billing, etcetera.

Organization should not be looked at as a stagnant, or one-time-only proposition. It is more like a garden. And needs constant attention. Weeds will grow without it. It requires such work as writing, typing, copying; listing, sorting, cataloguing, filing, cross filling, cutting, gluing, coding, stapling, coloring, and pulling the hair out of lour head.

It can also be compared to an old fashioned biplane, or a big jumbo jet. A biplane can be built quickly and with a small amount of material. It can take off and land in a cow pasture, and is very maneuverable. A big jumbo jet requires a huge amount of money, expertise, time, planning, material, and effort to build. Once built, it requires a very long, concrete runway in order take off and land. But it can travel great distances, and carry tremendous payloads. What do you want your organization to do for you? Do you want to make $20,000 a year? Then you need very little organizing.

Do you want to make $100,000 a year? Then you need a lot of organizing. Do you want to increase your current income by ten percent? Then you need just a little more organizing.

There are two common excuses for resisting efforts to organize. The most common is the fear of "over" organizing. This is really amusing. After many years in the business, I can recall less than five people who were actually over organized. If you afraid of becoming "over" organized, you are being a big baby and should knock it off. The second common reason for resistance is "to time." If you are happy with your current results, fine. If you want to earn more money, or if you want to spend less time making money, then you must make the time.

How to Organize

1. First, make a decision that you need it and want it.
2. Then make a decision that you are going to do something about it.
3. Then relax. Let those decisions sink in. Trust that you will be able to do it without having to be some super-duper genius. You are already capable of doing it. Whew! Feel better?
4. Organizing is such a big and important job that you want to break it down into "baby steps." Forget about any idea that starting next Monday morning you are going to magically become organized.
5. The first baby step is to take a look at your current level of organization. I hope this isn't too painful. If you work for a company ask for your supervisor's opinion. Spend at least a few days evaluating yourself.
6. Now that you have a clear picture, write down what you want to change, improve, or add. You must write this down. Only you can decide what to do, but you will have things like: improve client file, improve client follow-up, check into office with greater regularity, turn orders into office sooner, start a rolodex file, reorganize brief case, rearrange desk, etcetera.
7. Prioritize your list. Select tasks that are easiest to do first. This way you can see some results right away and will feel good about getting something done. You can also plan to do the things that will be the most useful.

8. Begin. Some of these jobs are merely time consuming, clerical functions. Make these tasks as pleasant as you can. When I worked for a large employment agency we had to completely rebuild our client files. It couldn't be done during the day because it would have been too disruptive. Even with twelve of us, the job would take many hours. None of us wanted to do it, but the department manager made it relatively pleasant. We took all the material to hit apartment, and he bought pizza, beer, and soft drinks, and played some good music. It took us a few evenings, but it was worth it. It made our jobs easier, more effective, and more profitable. Enlist anyone you can to help you with clerical functions, Try friends, relatives, or paid help. Make it fun if you can. But even if you can't, do it anyway.
9. When you get one job done, move on to the next. And the next. Please keep in mind that organizing takes time and energy. Your needs will probably change over the months and years. But, once you get on top of your organizing, you will find these changes are much easier to make.

Planning

"Day's are like raw material waiting for an architect to fashion a unique adventure"
                                E. James Rohn

So how have your days been going? How would you like them to go? It's up to you. If you don't have a plan, you'll fit into someone else's very nicely.

It has always amazed me how well some people plan parties, wedding, and trips to Europe, but allow their careers to just happen. These same people wonder why their daily live are boring, but have a blast at parties. It's a crazy world isn't it? Day planning is just too much trouble.

Plan your work and work your plan. People who fail to plan are planning to fail. The evidence is in gang, planning is effective. So what is all the resistance about? I have a theory. (That's why I asked the question. Remember, I am the author.)

Most of us who grew up in America where trained to work in offices, and fast food places. or to do some type of labor. Someone else planned all that work. Planning is done with your brain; therefore, it is not viewed as work. Thinking is a waste of time. Labor is work. If you are caught thinking, you are to be scolded and told to, "Do something!" You are accused of daydreaming, and reminded that an idle brain is the devil's workshop. Well surprise! Planning is work, and sometimes, hard work.

In addition to planning your day's work, you can plan one-time-only things such as building a new account, moving into management, learning a skill, or a special presentation. One of the best things about planning is this is where you get to use your imagination. Imagine what you could accomplish every day. Imagine how you could build that new account. Imagine how you could become a manager or owner of your own business.

There are times when we do not know what to do. The trick here is to learn to admit that. Some people would rather eat raw snails than to admit, "I don't know what to do next." If you want to learn how to plan you days, here are three suggestions:

1. Go to an office supply store and select a good day-planner.
2. Write down a few things each day that you are going to do, ever if they seem incredibly obvious. Get in the habit of writing these things down each and every day. This is the key. Day planning is entirely too difficult to expect to do well, quickly. By developing the daily habit, you will then be able to expand the amount and complexity of daily tasks.
3. Learn to prioritize. The ABC method is very popular and very good. Write an A, B, or C nest to each task you have listed.

    "A" is for your most important tasks. A good way to decide "A" activities is to ask, "Does this make me the most money?" If it does, then list an A next to that task.

"B" is for moderately important tasks.
"C" is for simple, non-critical tasks.

This will get you started. There is a lot of good material written about this subject. It really takes very little effort to actually learn how to do it. The hard part is in the doing. Planning is necessary for earning lots of money. It is also necessary if you want permanent, lifetime employment, even for ordinary amounts of money. It is a good idea for everyone to plan. But, they don't

Another thing to do is to prepare. Make sure you have all of your materials with you when you work, whether it's in the office or in the field. Include even the most basic items, like yellow pads, pens, and gasoline for your car. Whenever you are going to get in your car and visit a client, make sure you know the directions, and have the phone number with you in case of a delay. For those of you who already do this, I can hear you laughing at the mention of something so obvious. But remember, you had to learn it at the beginning too. As funny as it may seem, it costs professional sellers millions and millions of dollars ever year. And there is simply no reason for it.

Larry Yslas

Numbers

Selling is a numbers game. How many prospects can you contact? How many can you close? How many buyers can be repeated? This is where all the analysis comes in. It doesn't matter whether you are a large, multi-national conglomerate, or a small, door-to-sales person, you have some numbers to keep track of and analyze.

Why? Numbers are the way sellers control quality. When I began my career as an employment consultant, I had to make ten presentations in or to get a sale. That was good, but I want to do better. With experience I go it down to six presentations to make a sale. Still not good enough. I studied harder and got that down to four presentations to make a sale. Then after four years, I got that number down to less than two.

For those of you who sell directly, on a daily basis, you need to control the quality of your daily production. This is a very, very, important set of numbers. Many business and individuals don't keep daily production number, and it keeps quality low. Far too many sellers only count sales. The reason this is a mistake is that sales are the result of some specific work. This subject requires some hard thinking. Because every one of you has a different situation, I can only give you guidelines.

There are usually between two and five functions that sellers perform daily that are critical to the production of sales. Some possibilities:

1. Total calls or contacts of some kind, whether in person or on the phone, regardless of results. It is only the number of attempts. In retail, this may mean total numbers of walk-in traffic.
2. Total number of contacts qualified. In other words, how many of the total contacts are actually interested and able to buy?
3. The number of presentations you make.
4. The number of hours you spend on various tasks.
5. The amount of time spent on developing new accounts

I hope this gives you a good idea of what kind of numbers to keep track of every day.

The way to keep track of numbers is up to you. There are excellent computer software programs available. For my daily numbers I simply use a 31-day column sheet. Each day I write down my production. I sub-total the weekly and monthly. Over the months you will have a crystal clear picture of what you need to keep doing, and what you need to change or improve.

Listening

Listening is one of the single most important skills for anyone interested in being a good seller. One of the most common myths about sellers is that they have to be good talkers. This is simply not true. It is listening that is required of those who sell well. Most people hear, but don't listen. That means they are not listening in an active way. Active? That's right. There is nothing passive about being a good listener.

How to become an active listener:
1. Pay attention to the person you are listening to. That person, and that person alone, whether it is a child, adult, family member, or business contact. We can all tell when someone is not paying attention to what we are saying, and it makes us feel small. When you listen to someone actively, whether on the phone or in person, they are the only person in the world for that moment. That makes people fell important. If you spend you time making people feel important, how can you lose?
2. Pay attention to the content of what is being said. Everyone has a different problem. To each person that problem is equally important. A high school girl with a sick horse is feeling just as much pain as a business executive with a sick business. Never underestimate how people feel about what they say. It is the job of the active listener to ask questions that lead to understanding the content of what is

being said. Ask open-ended questions that begin with who, what, when, where, why, and how.
3. Evaluate, don't judge. Good listeners learn to stay away form the judgmental words like good, bad, right, and wrong. Learn a professional detachment. A doctor wants to cure a patient of cancer even though he told that patient to stop smoking cigarettes ten years earlier. And the patient wants to be cured, not preached at. If you are selling safety belts you are not going to get very far by telling your prospects they are stupid for not using them. However, if you inquire about their thinking on safety, you may be in a position to demonstrate that your product could save a life. See the difference? Besides, being judge of the universe is a heavy burden.
4. Take notes. This increases your effectiveness as a listener to a large degree. It frees your memory. It reduces the possibility of mistakes. It allows you to give more, and therefore, sell more. Most people love it when you write down things they are saying.
5. Learn to love silence. Silence drives most people crazy. Maybe this is why people think you have to be a good talker. They think silence is a bad thing. Not true. Silence is very powerful. Most people are so afraid of silence that they listen too fast. They think there should be no space between the end of one sentence and the beginning of another.

Here are two "silent" ideas that will dramatically increase your selling power.

First, allow three beats of silence before responding to what a person says to you. I promise you will be shocked at how much of life you have been missing by taking three beats worth of silence before you speak. Not three seconds, just three imaginary taps of your toe. Two things happen. One, you have more time to say or ask something intelligent. Two, you discover that a great deal of the time the person you listening to will keep talking over the three beats. If there is any magic in this book, it is how much you will learn while people keep on talking. More often than not, it is here that they will reveal what they truly want. Try it!

Second, whenever you lose the attention of anyone you are talking to, close your mouth and wait. Do this in person, or on the phone. Wait patiently. Don't' sound disgusted or punitive. This idea will actually amuse you when you see how effectively it works. And it works on absolutely everyone. Don't be intimidated by business executives. They appreciate it when you wait patiently while they are distracted. They respect you more. This is especially effective when someone is trying to do two things at once. Since you are willing to give your complete attention, you should now demand the same. When I talk to someone and they are not able to give me their full attention, I simply ask for a better time to call jack. Talking to people who are not willing to cooperate with you is a serious waste of your time.

Observation

The value of observation. Pay attention! Professional sellers cannot survive long without looking both ways before crossing the street to make sales. They get run over. Just as it is important to develop listening skills, it is important to develop your observation skills. The universe is a huge place and cannot be "seen" with just a passing glance.

This is a nice, easy subject. All you have to do is develop the habit of spending a little more time looking at what you see before you. Just because it's easy, don't pass it by. I bring this subject up because it can be a fabulous source of new buyers, or new products or services.

Did you ever hear of the Holiday Inn hotel chain? A gentleman from Tennessee who wanted to take his family on a trip across the state started it. When he began looking for places to spend the night he found only cheap, dirty motels, or wonderful, but expensive, hotels. He observed there were no medium priced, clean, simple places for a middle class family. That was shortly after World War II. Today we have not only the Holiday Inns, but also numerous motels for middle-income families.

When I was an employment consultant I found jobs for professionals in the computer industry. Like most people who begin a new job, I had to work very hard to get new business. Remember, the experienced sales staff already took the obvious and easy business. I made a rather profitable observation of company called

IBM. (You may have hard of them.) My observation was of a new line of computer they had just developed. No one else paid any attention besides me. Well, I cleaned up. I saw a major new market within an old, existing market.

Become an active looker. See what people are wearing. Look at the colors. Look at the styles. See the expressions of the faces of people you come in contact with. When you walk into an office of a client, look at the walls. What's on them? Are they blank? Do they have pictures of their families? You can tell a lot by looking. You can tell if the person is well organized, just by looking. You can tell if the person is open- minded, just by looking.

A great way to stimulate your observation skills is to periodically take a new way to work. Do that tomorrow, even if you have to take a little extra time. You will be pleased at what you see. Don't let your life get into a rut. There is a great world out there. Take a look.

Telephones

Everyone has a phone. At home, at work, in cars, and now, even in restaurants. Do not overlook the advantages of this kind of contact. I have made more that 500,000 business calls in my career. There is no way I could have contacted that many people making personal visits. That is why I took my job as an employment consultant. I wanted an inside sales job. I took a good look at selling real estate, but I decided to get a job where I had more control over the amount of prospecting I could do. No one pays you for waiting in traffic jams. If you are on the phone and you client is out, you can make another call within a few seconds. Also, you are available for incoming calls when you are sitting at your desk, rather than the lobby of some client.

These days the advantages are so well known that even those with outside sales jobs can use the telephone to enhance most phases of work.

Telephone contact is just as personal and intimate as in person contact. Maybe more. The tone of voice can determine the tone of the contact. You can be exited or calm. You can be friendly or business-like. You can chat or gather important information. I can tell what kind of mood my clients are in by the way they sound. I can tell if they're busy. When a client is busy, I usually do one of two things: state my business in as brief a manner as possible, or ask when it would be best to call back.

When you talk to someone on the phone it doesn't matter how you are dressed. When I have to make a lot of phone calls I just where shorts or Levis. I know of some people who take the phone out by their swimming pool or a balcony overlooking the ocean. Doesn't that sound like a great way to do business? There are also those who just feel more business-like if they wear a complete business suit or outfit.

Another advantage of using the telephone is scheduling. It is very easy to arrange call backs based on the client's schedule. If they are in their office early in the morning, call then. If late afternoon is their best time, call then. I almost never ask clients to return my calls. I would rather place the call. That way, I am prepared. When you ask a client to call you back, they have a knack of calling at the worst possible time. You have to put them on hold, wade through a mountain of paperwork, and then, if they are still waiting, talk to them.

If you have not been using the telephone, do yourself a favor and consider some of these advantages. If you have been avoiding the phone because it scares you, remember that repeated use will make you more skilled and more comfortable.

Questions

Quest. In search of. Pursuit. Experts in most professions are valued more by the questions they ask than the answers they give. In most cases, if we ask the right questions the answers are reduced to simplicity. This is true for most professional sellers.

When I interview a professional computer specialist, or an employer looking to hire a computer specialist, I ask more than 50 questions. When I am done with my questions I pretty much know what they want. It took me years to learn all those questions. They are based on many mistakes and many successes.

Make it your business to become effective at asking questions. There are two types of questions that are very important to sellers: open-ended and closed. Both are very valuable, but the difference can be critical. Open-ended question are the ones that begin with who, what, when, where, why, and how. (Are these starting to sound familiar? Closed questions are those that require a yes or a no. Experience and training will teach you when to use which.

As a rule, most of the questions you ask should be open-ended. Here are examples of how to ask questions both ways.

Closed: "You do want this luxury model, don't you?

Closed: "Do you want this luxury model?

Open: "What do you look for in a luxury model?

Open: What do you like best about this luxury model?

Open-ended questions usually deliver a lot more information. Use them when you want to probe. Closed questions are best when you want very specific information about whether to continue on a given subject. Remember, some prospects just love to talk without any serous intent to buy. So, periodically, a good yes or no question can help you stay on track. I like to ask questions like;" Does that make sense? Can you see yourself making a purchase like this? Do you ever make decisions on a first call?

An Introduction to Selling

Negotiating

To deal or bargain with. To arrange for or bring about by discussion and settlement of terms. That is how my dictionary defines negotiating. That doesn't seem so difficult, does it? Well, it's not.

Negotiating is largely a matter of common sense. You can negotiate anything. One of my earliest lessons as a seller was how to collect bills. A man owed a small advertising bill to the radio station I worked for. He owned a beauty salon and one day my boss was visiting his shop in order to collect. Well, it turned out that not only was he a shopkeeper, he was also a cat burglar. As my boss arrived he found the man being handcuffed and arrested by the police. While the police were locking up the shop my boss decided it was a good time to negotiate terms for payment. He simply asked the guy how he wanted to handle the payment. At that time prisoners were given small amounts of money each month to buy things like postage stamps or cigarettes. He agreed to send some of that money each month until his bill was paid. He kept is agreement.

I have never forgotten that story. I have always asked my clients how they want to pay me, rather than demand it. Consequently, I have never had any serious problems collecting my bills. (I have had some serious problems paying, but not collecting.)

You will always find people who want to negotiate price. That goes with the territory. But please remember, most of them really enjoy the process. Don't disappoint them. Try to avoid a simple yes or no upon their request. Come back with an offer of your own. Tell them you'll give them two of what they ask for at that lower price, or maybe throw in something extra.

Sometimes you will have to negotiate a deal for a broken product or fouled-up service. This can be very tricky. This is where you have to be quite diplomatic if you want to satisfy your customer and your own sense of value and fair play. Keep in mind that this is a process, and not set in stone, and you will do very well.

I recommend a book called You Can Negotiate Anything, by Herb Cohen, one of America's foremost negotiators. Presidents have called on him for help with international relations. In addition to being very informative, it is one of the funniest books I have ever read. There are other excellent books available on the subject.

Thinking

Intelligence and thinking are not the same. Intelligence has more to do with capacity and thinking has more to do with process. Thinking takes energy and time. Twenty five percent of the oxygen we take in goes to the brain. You will be tired physically after expending massive thought energy. Most people stop improving their thinking around the age of eight. I hope this sounds challenging. I know people who are more intelligent than I am who use their brains for practically nothing. One of the reason I enjoy selling is that when you use your brain you are rewarded. Anyone of you reading this book is capable of achieving any desired goals. Remember, most managers and company owners have a background in selling.

Never in the history of the world has one nation provided so much for so many. The founding fathers were some of the greatest thinkers ever on this planet. Thomas Jefferson gave us the idea that men were innocent until proven guilty, helped construct the Declaration of Independence, and invented the dumbwaiter. Benjamin Franklin gave us the idea for public libraries, public fire departments, and invented the lightening rod. They did not possess superior intelligence, but they were superior thinkers. If we want this nation to last another 200years, it will come form continued superior thinking.

If you have been hiding behind the idea that you are not very smart, stop it. If you have a real high I.Q., big deal. Thinking is what gets results. Reading is thinking. Writing is thinking. Daydreaming is thinking. Do lots of these things. Question ideas that you hear. There are many "sayings" that we hear throughout our lives. Some are truly wonderful. Some are truly stupid.

When I was twelve years old I got a dog. I taught him how to sit, speak, roll over, climb a ladder, and fetch. There was a saying that you couldn't teach an old dog new tricks. So I waited till my dog was old and I taught him how to sit up. You can teach an old dog new tricks.

Is anyone telling you that you can't? If so, go find those who think you can. Get around people who like to use their brains to accomplish something that you believe is worthwhile. This is a book about selling, but it's also true for other activities.

Think about it.

Intuition

"A hunch is creativity trying to tell you something."
...Frank Capra

Have you ever had a hunch? Of course you have. We all have an inner voice that goes beyond thinking, logic, or specific words. Intuition is something that we feel. We all have this inner voice, not just women. It is something that is wise to encourage.

My attitude toward selling is not to compete, but to create. Why worry about what the competition is doing? They are going to keep on doing it as long as they want to, and are able to. You have no control over them. You only have control over you. We live in an abundant universe. There is plenty of room at the top. It's the bottom that is crowded. If you have those hunches, or ideas for new products or services, you may be right. You may be wrong, too, so don't get cocky.

Intuition will warn against bad business decisions or impending danger. If you are entering into a business deal of some kind, and you have this vague feeling that something is wrong, something is probably wrong. Pay attention to those feelings. State them up front. Maybe you work for a large company and they want to promote you to regional sales manager and develop a whole new territory. Normally that would sound absolutely fabulous to you. But, your inner voice is telling you there is danger. Check it out. Ask questions. Don't go forward until you have resolved the issues that your inner voice is bringing up.

Larry Yslas

Words

There are approximately 500,000 words in the English language. The average college graduate knows 50,000 of them. Winston Churchill was said to have had a vocabulary of 200,000. The reason there are so many words is that they are very specific. English is such a precise language that people in non-English speaking countries use it to write business contracts.

English is a marvelous language. It is lively, colorful, and quite democratic. We can make up words anytime we like. How else could you come up with half a million? Most of the words during the last few decades have come from our space programs, science, and computers. When the last century began, Americans didn't have vocabulary words like jets, modems, or interferon. And, of course, jive turkey, punker, disco, and groovy would have drawn blank stares.

But the words we hear and use daily are the ones sales people need to be aware of. When I am reading and I come across an unusual word, such as spelunker, (a person who explores caves), I don't always look it up. I just don't have the time. I look up the words I use often. It can be very educational. There are several good dictionaries. I use the Random House College Dictionary. Here are some examples:

Enthusiasm. Lively, absorbing interest. Excited involvement.

This is a wonderful thing to have. If your heart is in your dream you will find yourself filled with it. You won't have to fake it, which is really good, because nothing is more pathetic than pretend enthusiasm. You will actually be enthusiastic. One of the best ways to build enthusiasm is to hang around others who are already enthusiastic. It can rub off of them and on to you. And vice versa.

Inspire. To infuse an animating, quickening, or exalting influence into.

There are times when you can inspire someone to buy your product or service. You just have to infuse an animated influence into them. (Do you see why it is easier to learn 20 closes?)

Perseverance. Steady persistence in a course of action. A purpose. Doggedness. Steadfastness.

This is a key element to success. This is how Thomas Edison was able to make an electric light. Remember how he felt on attempt number 5,456. How is your perseverance?

Persuade. To prevail on a person to do something. To induce to believe; convince.

One of the myths about selling is that you have to be persuasive. That would mean that you have to prevail on people. To convince people. Well, sometime you can indeed. But, by now you realize it is rarely necessary.

Manipulate. To handle, manage, or use, especially with skill, in some process of treatment or performance.

This word has gotten bad press. People usually use it in a negative way. But it is only negative if the intent is negative. We all manipulate others and need to be manipulated. It's called life.

Larry Yslas

These are just five words that are used frequently in the selling profession. Some of them are overrated and some are underrated. It is helpful to nitpick when you do something on a permanent, or daily basis. You don't have to have a large vocabulary to be good at speaking or writing, but you do need to use words accurately. Get friendly with your dictionary. Keep it where it is handy. If you don't have one, buy one. Or, if you have an old one, buy a new one. It is amazing how rapidly they become outdated.

Body Language

The way we carry ourselves says a whole lot about us. You probably have heard the expression, "Stand tall." That means look alive, stand up straight, and don't slouch. The amount of confidence you have in yourself really shows up in your physical appearance. People who walk slowly, and look as if they just got out of bed, do not inspire confidence. You can slouch when you are standing or when you are sitting. It is interesting that slouching comes through your voice over the telephone. People who look tired, usually sound tired. Many years ago at a seminar I learned that you should sit up straight and smile, even when talking on the telephone. It may seem strange to you, but try it the next time you are on the phone with a customer. It's amazing how true it is.

When you are meeting people in person, not only do you want to smile and stand up straight, be sure and look them in the eyes. Eye contact is another strong signal of self-confidence. Many of you younger readers, or those new to meeting people, may find this uncomfortable at first. A good way to learn to look at people in the eyes is to start by looking at their eyebrows or nose. Actually, it is impossible to look into both eyes at the same time. Eye contact is another very powerful tool. You will be surprised how uncomfortable you can make other people feel by staring at them in the eyes. In fact, politeness demands that you look away from time to time.

Whenever you ask someone a question, look them in the eyes. If they are lying, there is a good chance you can spot it at this moment. Really good liars can fool everyone, so this won't always be true. You can also tell how confident someone is by observing how he or she responds to your questions. Whenever some asks you a question, look them in the eyes. This signals to them that you are interested. This also lets them know that you are a self-confident person. Do this even if you don't know the answer. There is nothing wrong with not knowing every answer. We are human beings, not encyclopedias.

Body language tells you a lot about other people. If you are making a presentation to a prospect who is sitting there with arms folded, head drooping, and yawning occasionally, you have a very serious problem on your hands. The next time this happens, ask that person if you are boring them. They will probably straighten right up and you will make a sale. If you are actually boring them, you need to go find someone who is interested. If you are experiencing a lot of bored prospects you may need to jazz up your presentation.

Service

Service is one of the most endearing functions you can provide. And it doesn't matter whether you sell a product or a service. Lots of people really appreciate it when you attend to all of the details that go along with what you are selling. It is a good idea to look for those people as you do your prospecting and as you begin to develop repeat business. Buyers are not usually gong to tell you they appreciate it. In many cases they expect it. They may only bring it up when you fail to provide service.

There are many businesses today that make a lot of money by eliminating or drastically reducing service. Those huge discount houses that sell everything from toiletries to clothing are a good example. They have identified a very good market. They know that millions of people have already decided they want to buy Crest toothpaste. They don't want to try anything else. They just want to be able to get it in a very simple format. Well, once you can give them that, they are going to be very attracted to a low price. Doesn't that make sense?

But there are still lots of people who don't want to go to the K-Mart store. They want someone else to go to the store, buy the Crest toothpaste, and deliver it to their home. These are rich folks.

I wanted to point out those two extremes because most of us do a lot of our work in a vast middle area. Many of us are, indeed, middle persons. I work very hard at making my product or service very easy to use and to buy. Let me give you an example. When I was an employment consultant I had to arrange interviews between applicants and employers. I dealt with professional people who are quite capable of getting to an interview. Many of my fellow consultants would simply give their applicant the address and time, and let it go at that. But I would go to the trouble of finding out if my applicant already knew the exact location. Southern California is a very large place and much of the time they only had a vague idea of where they had to be. I would spend a few extra minutes of my time writing out detailed street and highway names and directions. I would tell them of landmarks to look for. I would tell them of the traffic conditions they would be likely to encounter. I would tell them not just the time they had to arrive at the interview, but what time they had to leave their home or office.

This seemed like such a small detail that most sellers didn't do it. But, look at the rewards. It was rare for me to have applicants show up late for an interview. Also, think for a moment about what goes on in someone's mind before going to a job interview. Most people are nervous to begin with. Having to drive to strange new places in strange new traffic conditions really adds anxiety. So instead of showing up exhausted on an interview, after getting lost or being late, or both, my applicants showed up relaxed and ready to get a great new job.

There are many of these little details that exist for nearly everyone who sells. Don't look at them as a thorn in your side. Look at them as an opportunity to increase your business. You will be rewarded in more ways than money. I feel very good when I help someone get a new job that really turns him or her on. I feel very good when someone calls me up and says, "Larry, I'm calling you because I need a better job and my friend says you are the best." Think about how you feel when you get those kinds of responses. Think about how good you feel when someone provides you with really good service. Hotels are very well known for providing really great service. A friend of mine once checked into a hotel only to discover he had a missing piece of luggage. That was really bad news. But, the people at the hotel called the airport for him, tracked down the luggage, picked it up, and delivered it to his room. That is service.

Larry Yslas

Stories

Once upon a time...
Long ago, and far away...
It was a dark and stormy night...

Everyone loves a good story. They always have, and they always will. Storytelling is a power tool. Stories achieve a great deal. They make things clear and understandable. They help the memory. They arouse emotions. They make us laugh. They make us cry. They make us think. They make us sign on the dotted line.

Some people are naturally good storytellers. They can make a trip to the supermarket sound like a fascinating adventure. It is a truly wonderful gift. If you are one of these people, capitalize on it. However, even if you are not one of these people, you can probably tell a few simple stories.

Since this is a book about selling, I am not talking about casual stores for the sole purpose of entertaining customers. I am talking about stories that have to do with work. Everyone has a story. There are millions of them. Rather than shower a prospect with a ton of adjectives about how great your product or service is, tell a story about it. "Mr. And Mrs. North bought this product last year and ever since then they have lived happily." The problem with adjectives is they are just your opinion. But, if Mr. and Mrs. North actually used your product and got results, it is clearer and more believable. People can relate to a story. If they are experiencing the same problems as the North family, they can relate to their story.

Another way to look at stories is to see them as painting pictures with words. Maybe you are a real estate agent and you have a beautiful home to sell. You can run down a list of features:

It has 5,000 square feet.
It has four bedrooms.
It has fruit trees in the back yard.
It has a fireplace.
Or, you can paint some word pictures.

"There is plenty of space, Mr. and Mrs. Prospect, so you will feel lots of freedom. You have plenty of room for your hobbies or for entertaining guests. You can turn this room into a nursery if you decide to have a family. In the spring you can pick your own fresh fruit for canning. On cold winter nights you can snuggle up together in front of the fireplace. You can listen to the romantic sounds of a crackling fire and rain falling gently on the roof."

Which of the two methods do you think is going to have the greater impact? Naturally, it's the picture painting approach. Not only is the effect gong to be greater, it is going to be a lot greater.

Storytelling is something you can work on. This is a moneymaker. I believe you can increase your income in a dramatic way by taking the time and making the effort to learn how to tell stories. All you have to do is begin to listen for them. When you hear a good story make a note of it. Start telling simple stories when you get the chance. Rather than placing a lot of pressure on yourself to tell stories in a professional situation, you may find it helpful to start in social settings. Tell stories at home, or with friends, or at parties. Make this a fun project.

Begin with stories from your own life. This is the most common advice you well hear about telling good stories. (Professional writers learn this early on.) Everyone did something interesting when they were in school. Maybe you won a national spelling bee. Vacations are a great source of stories. Maybe you had a trip to the mountains and you got snowed in. These stories don't have to be significant or earth shattering.

The best advice I've ever read on how to tell stories comes from Lewis Carroll, who wrote Alice in Wonderland. He said, "Start at the beginning. Go all the way to the end. Then stop.

Analogies

When it comes to making things clear, analogies are as important as stories. My dictionary defines an analogy as a partial similarity between like features of two things, on which a comparison may be based: the analogy between the heart and a pump.

As professionals, we grow extremely familiar with our products and services. It is very important for us to remember that our customer may be new, and unfamiliar, with the material we are presenting to them. With the use of analogies, we can make comparisons they can relate to.

There is a good analogy used by insurance sellers to demonstrate the differences in the costs of premium payments. They'll ask the prospect to consider a marble, a baseball, and basketball. If the prospect purchases insurance early in life, the premium is as easy as carrying a marble in their pocket or purse. If the prospect waits till mid-life, the premium is more like having to carry a baseball. It can be done, but it's more difficult and noticeable. Of course a basketball is a real problem. That really makes the point clear.

Another good analogy is the one where the seller says to a dairy farmer, "Just six bales of hay per month will make the payment on this new equipment." Raw dollar figures can be difficult to swallow. A dairy farmer knows the cost of six bails of hay in a more familiar way. It is easy to relate to.

Here are some old analogies: crazy as a loon, black as pitch, deader than a doornail, nuttier than a fruitcake, smooth as silk.

I use analogies for myself. It helps my own thinking. Earlier, I compared organizing to a biplane and a jumbo jet. I used that analogy because that is how I saw it a few years ago. I realized that size played a very crucial role in matters of organization.

Everyone can learn to make effective analogies. It's easy. Get out the old yellow pad and start writing. This is a good idea for a sales meeting or workshop.

Visual Aids

Visual aids can be very helpful. Business cards are probably the most common visual aid used among professional sellers, but they are usually given very little thought. We have all seen hundreds, if not thousands, of business cards. The most commonly used part is the telephone number, but it is nearly always in little tiny print. I always select big bold print for the phone number. So few people put any thought into their business cards that it is quite easy to come up with an idea or format that will attract attention. Take a look at your own business card and you will see what I mean.

T-shirts are one of my favorite visual aids. They can be used for cleverly worded sayings, or artistic logos or symbols. In addition, there are baseball caps, pens, balloons, matchbooks, stationery, calendars, and jackets. These are often referred to as novelty or promotional items. They are excellent ways to advertise and promote your products or services.

Visual aids can also be very useful for those of you who have to make major presentations. If you have a presentation that last more than just a few minutes, and is normally just a lot of hard information, you may want to consider visual aids to keep it lively and interesting. You can color it, or break it into segments to make the information easier to digest. You can use photographs and artwork with the same kind of effect as a magazine or newspaper. You can use charts and graphs. It's a good opportunity to use sample products, or any kind of gadget, to break up the monotony of dry words.

I know a radio advertising sales person who once wrote out his presentation on five extra large playing cards. He made his presentation "unfold" like a poker hand, with the prospect being the winner, of course. To really spice it up he wore a dealer's visor and garter on his arm. This pitch was to a major radio station owner who was notorious for hating salesmen. He won the account.

One girl sent a job resume in a cookie tin from Mrs. Field's cookies. One man once wanted to work for David Sarnoff, who built NBC. He sent him a pigeon in a little cage with a note attached, "If you would like to talk to someone clever enough to get your attention, take the pigeon to the window and let it out of its cage. He will tell me of your decision." According to the story, he got a job.

Methods

A method is a system or plan. There are methods to selling. Many years ago, after I had already been selling for a few years, is when I learned to sell methodically. I attended a major, three-day seminar called The Guaranteed Close. At first, I didn't even realize it was a method. I just thought I was taking another seminar on closing.

The Guaranteed Close is a seven-step method that I have never stopped using. The thing about selling by a method that is so exiting is that it permits the seller to always know what to do, what not to do, and what to do next. Before I learned to sell methodically I basically just reacted to whatever happened. It was the buyers who were in charge, not me.

Do you feel that way about selling? It is that problem that is the crux of this whole book. I have attended seminars that have taught me a lot. I have been to seminars that have left me feeling very excited. But when I lift that seminar I felt incredibly exited for two solid weeks, and I worked on the material for more than a year. For the fist time in my career in selling I felt like I was in charge, and I liked it. I still like it.

There are other methods. They seem to be gaining in popularity. One method I looked at in depth is called the Sandler Selling System. It looks good to me. The only reason I didn't try it is that I have one already. You will see methods advertised here and there and I strongly suggest you investigate the idea. Remember, of course, they take a considerable effort to learn and to implement. Once learned, however, they are like having extra horsepower. If you would like to check out The Guaranteed Close, contact Max Sachs International. They are listed under sales training in the business-to-business yellow pages for Los Angeles County

Persuasion

Persuading is convincing. The best way to be convincing is to be convinced. How do you feel about hour product or service? Are you convinced it is the best? Are you convinced that is just average? Buyers pick up on your feelings much more than they pick up on your words. Did you know that? It is very important to learn.

There is a saying, "Buyers convinced against their will, are of the same opinion still." Sales people can be very persuasive. But, if you just badger prospects, they will agree with you just to get you off their back, off the phone, out of their office, or out of their home. The most important point to learn about being persuasive is that it mainly works when the prospect already wants what you have to sell. Politicians are masters at this concept.

As a selling tool, persuasion is terribly overrated. The only reason I have included it is that so many people think it is the main key to selling. It isn't.

Scripting

There are many things that professional sellers say over and over again. They range form the approach we use to the way we say goodbye. Adlibbing, or "winging" it, is as effective for a sales person as it is for an actor. Writing out intelligent, will-planned scripts is one of the most valuable communication tools available.

Learning 20 closes is nothing more than memorizing 20 short scripts. The have already been written. Best of all, they have already been tested. So, what new script do you need for yourself? To determine this will require some thought. The first things you want to look at are those subjects that come up with some kind of regularity.

If you sell in a retail store you have to approach shoppers regularly. The most common script is, "May I help you?" Now it gets complicated. The shopper may have several different responses. Such as:

"I just want to browse."
"No thanks."
"No, not now."
"I'm not really sure."
"Well, I am just looking for ideas."
"Yes, I need some information."
"Yes, I want to buy…"

Well-trained professionals need to have a script for every single one of these responses. The way to do this is to get out that yellow pad and write down each response. Then write down at least two things to say. Examples:

"I'm sorry, but we don't allow browsing in this store. Just kidding!"

"Great, please browse as long as you like. If you need help, please ask."

"Wonderful, we welcome browsers. But, may I first show you this special item? It isn't listed in our advertising and I want to make sure you don't overlook it."

"That's fine. Was there something special you were looking for?"

Do you see the value here? Scripting allows you to be completely prepared for your buyers. There are times when they don't know what they want. The seller's job is to find out. Scripting allows for maximum opportunities. Scripting is something you can do on your own, or in group workshops or sales meetings.

Rehearsing. All of the techniques in the world are of no value if you don't know them well enough to use in front of a prospect. Reading books or attending seminars alone, will, not do the job. Remember professional singers. They now the words so well, they don't have to hum.

John Wooden was coach of the UCLA bruin basketball team for many years. He is one of the most successful coaches ever in the history of sports. I once saw him on local television being interviewed by a sportscaster. The interviewer wanted to know how much coach Wooden enjoyed the thrill of victory during those big games. He was surprised by the coach's response. Wooden said that it was during the practice sessions that the team won ball games. That is where he got his greatest satisfaction.

The same thing is true for selling. Don't look at rehearsing as a big drag. It is where you will win sales. It is where you develop skill. It is where you can grow as a professional. Give it time. Make an effort.

The best places to rehearse are where you won't be disturbed. Home is good. The car is good for making driving time useful. I must confess that at first I was a little embarrassed when someone in another car would catch me talking to myself. But I decided that I would rather improve my life than to worry about the opinion of a perfect stranger. Other good places to practice out loud are parks, lakes, or by the ocean.

The Voice

Speech is an "overlaid" function. What that means is everything that makes up our voice comes from something else. The vocal cords control air for eating and breathing. Teeth are for chewing. The lips are for sucking. The tongue is for tasting and for insulting idiots.

We hear our own voices differently than those around us do. That is why most of us hate to hear ourselves on tape recordings. If you feel that your voice quality could use some improvement, you are probably right. But, don't look for public speaking or English classes to solve this problem. Take those classes for improving the content of what you want to communicate.

Speech therapists and pathologists can help voice quality problems. They can usually be found in the yellow pages, or on college or university campuses. There are some good books available, too.

Here are some problems that occasionally come up:

Sore throats. If you are experiencing a lot of them and your doctor doesn't quite know why, it could be a matter of speech mechanics.

General strain. Do you feel like you are always straining? The voice should feel comfortable at all times, even if you talk all day, every day.

Pitch. Is your voice too high or too low?

Heavy dialect. Especially foreigners, but regional dialects can be a problem, too.

Speech impediments these can be eliminated or at least controlled.

Breathing problems. Your voice may have an airy or breathy quality. (Sort of like Marilyn Monroe.) It may be too weak or soft, or too strong or loud.

Speed. You can learn to slow down or speed up.

Poor articulation. Are people always asking you to repeat yourself?

Too nasal. This means you talk through your nose. You can learn to use your chest and oral cavities to enrich the sound of your voice.

You may simply want to improve the over quality of the sound or tone of your voice. This is a good idea. Why not have a more pleasing sound? It can help you in expressing yourself. For this improvement, you may also take voice lessons from a vocal coach. They specialize in both singing, and public speaking. Go for it.

An Introduction to Selling

Communications

Communication. How well do you relate to the people in your life? Your customers, co-workers, supervisors, managers, friends, family, strangers. Don't answer this question quickly. Think about this over a long period of time. Your ability to communicate with other human beings has a dramatic impact on your life.

Sometimes very intelligent, very competent, very nice people get absolutely nowhere in their careers because they cannot communicate effectively with others. This is not an unusual problem.

This is a tough and tricky issue. How do you know? I suggest you ask around. Ask your supervisor. Ask your co-workers. I suggest you look at where you are, versus where you would like to be. Are you getting as many new sales or accounts as you want? Do you get the promotions you want? Do you get invited to the business and social events you want? Do you find yourself arguing with people? Do people tell you that you don't listen? If you ask these questions, you will find the answers. And, if you are not so good at communicating, you will be able to improve.

By getting better at some of the tools of your trade, you will automatically become better at communicating with others, especially if you become better at listening and storytelling.

How would you like to become instantly better at talking or public speaking? This easy little tip will do it. Guaranteed.

Larry Yslas

Make a list of what you want to say; whether you are making a callback to a client, a proposal to your boss, a request of your spouse, or addressing the local PTA, You don't have to be eloquent, or memorize anything. You just have to know what it is that you want to say. Here is what a good list might look like.

-new contest
-pricing structure
-idea for automobile mileage
-need to improve street flooding
-love the way your hair looks
-need feedback about new air conditioning system

A list can have one thing or it can have 20. The point is to write down a word or phrase to represent each idea that you wish to communicate. As you express each one, take a pen and cross it off. When they are all crossed off, stop. I hope this helps you.

An Introduction to Selling

PART FOUR

THE SIXTH BASIC ELEMENT

SELLERS

"Not in the clamor of the crowded street, not in the shouts and plaudits of the throng, but in ourselves are triumph and defeat."
...Henry Wadsworth Longfellow

A Career in Selling

There are many reasons for choosing a career in selling.

Money is one. As a group, professional sellers are among the highest paid people in the world. When you drive around beautiful neighborhoods filled with those expensive homes, professional sellers own many of them. They can make a lot of money. But a lot of money may not be what you have in mind. Most of you who are reading this book do not really want to lot of money. Having lots of money is only a big deal to some people. When you own a huge home, you have to hire gardeners, housekeepers, accountants, and the like. And, not only do you have to deal with all these people, you have to maintain this life style.

Some people take this route. Instead of making lots of money in total, make money in a few hours, or a few months, and then stop. Some make enough to maintain a nice apartment or a small home and then have lots of time. Time for you. Time for your family. Time for your hobbies. Time for art. You fill in the rest. Isn't this a great idea? I believe too many people think of money only in terms of a grand, annual total.

From a career standpoint you are wise to think of it from different angles. Maybe you just want a simple, dependable job that pays average amounts of money. If that is what you want, do not let anybody talk you out of it. Maybe you don't want to take all those seminars and do all that studying. You are not going to get any flack from me. In fact, this book is written to do you some real good if you read no other book. That's why this book is short and easy to read. For some reason, those people who want to make a lot of money think that everyone wants to make a lot of money. I must confess that I used to think that myself. I only learned otherwise after a couple of years as an employment consultant.

Do you like to run things? More than half of all upper level management comes from the ranks of sales people. I am talking about power positions like owners and presidents. The next largest source group is accountants, and they are only six percent of the total. So, if you are interested in being in charge, selling is the ticket.

Why is this so? I know of three important reasons. First, sellers deal with making and getting decisions on a professional basis every single day. People who run things have to make and get decisions. It is a skill. This is a purely practical fact of life. Second, sellers have to learn more about how a company works than any other single member of the staff. When I say more about a company, I really mean everything. Third, they generate the income that pays the bills and everyone's salary. A company can have the greatest product or service in the world, but if they have no sellers, they have no income. Conversely, good sellers can sell weak products and services.

Another important thing to keep in mind about selecting a job for the purpose of running things is to learn where the jobs are. Big corporations get big press, but they only hire about twenty percent of the work force. Small business provides more than half of the jobs. That is where I like it. I hate working for big companies. But, it is purely a matter of personal taste. I made a lot of money because of IBM and I have the utmost respect for the company.

Independence. There are few occupations with as much potential for independence as selling. Most people need to work with others in a group of some kind. But, there are lots of others who want to set their own hours, dress the way the like, come and go without question or observation, and generally call their own shots. This can be achieved in this profession. You can also find a combination of the two. Many companies have very loose arrangements with their sales representatives. The difficulty that arises is learning how to sell when you are completely by yourself. I personally recommend that you first work for a company with a structured sales staff. Then, after you have leaned the craft, move into more independent positions.

Security is another advantage that comes with selling. If you keep your selling skills current, you can usually find a job somewhere.

Comfort and convenience. You can sell from your own home.

There you have a few reasons to choose selling as a career. I'm sure you have reason of your own. I hope that this book will encourage many people to enter the field.

There are so many different ways to get started selling that I could not possibly cover them all. So, I will give you a couple of ideas to get you going and a few of the pitfalls to consider. There is a downside to this business, and you are better off knowing them.

The best advice I can give you is true for any profession you might want to enter. Talk to people who are already doing it. If you want to sell computers, talk to several computer sales people. If you want to sell yachts, talk to yacht sales people. This advice is also true for changing companies or changing your product or service. Make sure you talk to several people If you have not yet selected your product or service, talk to a variety of sales people. It is important to talk to at least three or four experienced people. One thing that may happen is that one of them may offer you a job. But, if it's only the first or second person you talk to, don't accept the job till you have completed your task. Tell the person you will consider the offer, and go talk to additional professionals.

The second piece of advice I have for getting started, or for changing direction within the field, is to read a book titled, What Color Is Your Parachute, by Richard Bolles. This excellent book provides you with all the information and instruction you need.

This brings up pitfall number one, blue-sky. This is a treacherous problem. Professional sellers are not usually trained how to hire people. They feel they have to paint this absolutely glorious picture of what it is like to work for them. The problem is they are sincere. They believe this is the way to hire. When you are talking to these people make sure you ask about the downside. Another important point to keep in mind is that you are exploring the field or the company. Do not go in with a hidden agenda of getting hired. It can backfire. You need information, not blue-sky. This is a widespread problem, so beware.

Pitfall number two is management. Have you heard that good help is hard to find? While that is sometimes true, the really difficult thing to find is good management. I can tell you this after dealing with hundreds of managers for well over a decade. Managing is a skill. More importantly, managing is a completely different skill. Far too many people are promoted into management positions without an ounce of training or education.

There is a significant difference between supervising and managing. Supervisors oversee work. Managers set policy and make decisions. I get a lot of flack when I tell people this. They don't like to hear it. But, I learned it after running my own company for a few years. I can't give you more details here, but if you are interested in upper level management, or owning your own business, I urge you to give it some thought.

This next pitfall is very tricky. It has to do with the early part of your career. Selling is a technical occupation. You need to learn a wide variety of techniques. It is rare to learn all that you need at one or two companies. My advice is to change jobs after two or three years during the early part of your career. If you stay too long with one company, your income may rise to a level that you cannot maintain should you make a move. In other words, you are stuck with that company. If you are currently stuck in a company at a high-income level, here is how you break out. You must realize there some pain and sacrifice ahead. Then, begin to cut back on your living expenses and start a savings account. You need to have enough saved up to live for one full year with no income. (Actually, everyone in the field of selling is wise to have a one-year savings account.) Next, do as I have already suggested and start talking to other sales people about making a change. In the meantime, take a lot of training seminars and learn about new companies, products, and services to prepare you for a major career move.

Another major pitfall is the ever-changing marketplace. There is no such thing as absolute job security. It simply does not exist. It doesn't exist for farmers, steelworkers, teachers, or sellers. When this country began 200 years ago, more than 90 percent of the work force consisted of farmers. Today it is two percent. Not one company that was in the fortune 500 at the beginning of the last century is around today. The marketplace is not fixed.

Here is a common scenario: You take a job with a company selling widget cleaners. You work very hard and at the end of the year your are making two thousand dollars a month. The market for widget cleaners begins to take off and by the end of the second year your are making five thousand dollars a month. You start buying things like new clothes, a car, a television set and a VCR. You begin eating in better restaurants, attending sporting events, going to concerts, taking trips, and living the good life.

Very quietly, and without your awareness, other people begin to enter the marketplace with new versions of widget cleaners that are less expensive and have some unique features. However, by the end of the third year you are making ten thousand dollars a month. You buy your first dream home and are committed to large monthly payments. You are now hooked on ten thousand dollars a month and believe you need more.

During the fourth year sales begin to level off. Unfortunately, your spending does not. You begin to borrow money. Your company begins to react to this new competition by cutting prices and commissions. Things begin to fall apart, but you are not yet feeling the pain.

During the fifth year your sales actually begin to fall and you decide it is time to change jobs. You begin looking at jobs that pay fifteen thousand dollars a month. But, any job that pays that much requires that you start at the bottom. It requires six months to a year at only five thousand dollars a month, and you cannot afford that.

Now your company loses some of it sales staff and you are given a larger territory. Not only is your income shrinking, but also you have more work to do. You begin to have family problems. You begin to feel the pain. You begin to lose your selling skills. Finally, you lose your job.

You learn that your value on the open market is less than you thought. Your ten thousand dollar-a- month value was only at the widget cleaning company, and only under certain market conditions. Those conditions are gone forever.

Do you get the picture? This is not an unusual story. There is nothing wrong with getting into a company and making big money. The trick is to learn how to deal with it. Don't get hooked on a big income that is temporary in nature. Don't misinterpret the marketplace. If you do, admit it. Admit you messed up. Then go at it again. Here is a question to write down on a card and place where you will see it periodically: "If I lost my job, what is my value on the open market today?"

I hope telling you about the downside of selling doesn't scare you away. I hope you will use this information as a source of strength rather tan fear. I hope you can better focus on the reasons that are good about this profession.

1. You can earn a good about of money.
2. You can set your own hours and control the total amount of work time.
3. You can run things.
4. You can achieve independence.
5. You can achieve a reasonable amount of income security.
6. You can achieve comfort and convenience.

Goals

"Give us the luxuries of life, and we will dispense with its necessaries"

...Oliver Wendell Holmes, Sr.

This is the part of the book just for those of you who want the luxuries of life and are willing to make an effort. This is for those of you who insist on success. Get a yellow pad because the worst possible place to keep you goals is in your head. I have made a very intensive study of high achievers from all walks of life and nearly all of them write their goals down on paper.

Having goals and plans is like having a destination and a map. What is your career destination? What do you want to be doing in five years, or ten years? Let me suggest some ideas.

You can become an expert at just about anything in five years. How would you like to be an expert sales person in five years?

Continue selling, but increase your value. For example, you can move up from selling small quantities of office supplies to small businesses, to selling large quantities of office supplies to large businesses.

Continue selling, but increase your value by increasing the value of your market. For example, you can sell radio advertising in a small-town market, then a medium sized market, and then a major market like New York, Chicago, or Los Angeles.

Continue selling, but increase your value by increasing the size of your product or service. For example, you can become a real estate agent selling homes valued at less than $150,000, then homes valued at up to $500,000, and then homes valued at over a million dollars. Not easy, but it has been done.

An Introduction to Selling

Move into management. Select a company large enough to offer management positions. If you are in a hurry, I suggest you choose one with a lot of turnover. However, this is a lot like walking into a minefield.

Go into business for yourself. If you already know what product or service you want to deal in, choose a company that specializes in that. If you \don't know, choose any good company. In both cases, start saving money.

Those are some good ideas. You may have some of your own.

It is also very important to write down your money goals. It isn't useful to write down vague terms like, "lots of money" You need to be specific. The best way to arrive at a figure is to determine your desired lifestyle. Write down the things you want to do, and to own, in great detail. A house can cost anywhere form $50,000 to many millions. The price of the home you want will depend on location, size, material, etc. Write the details down, calculate the amount, and then write down the price. Traveling costs depend on where you want to go, how you want to get there, and what you want to do when you arrive. Write down your travel goals, calculate the cost, and write them down. Do this for all of your goals.

Now that you have written down your goals, including dollar amounts, the next step is to read them every day. If you would like more details about how to set goals, read the book Think And Grow Rich, by Napoleon Hill.

Finally, your goals are written on paper, not stone. It is OK to change your mind. A great side benefit to writing them down is spontaneity. Because you have a direction in life, you will be able to take those nice spontaneous side trips that fate serves up. When you do achieve your goals, reward yourself. Feel very good about your success. You deserve the best. Keep in mind, however, that these feelings may fade and you will need to repeat this process. I wish you the very best. As Mae West once said, "Too much of a good thing is wonderful."

Self Image

> "Money, and responsibility, and prestige don't mean anything if they take away your ability to feel good about yourself."
> Dr. David Viscot

How do you feel about yourself? I would like your answer to be that you feel good, because if not, it is going to be more difficult to give your best performance. Remember, to the degree that you give others what they want, they will give you what you want. If you don't feel good about yourself, you won't be able to give freely. You will hold back. You won't feel complete.

Feeling good about yourself permits you to give the most you are capable of giving. By giving the most, you will receive the most. Remember, there is reciprocity in selling. We give and we get. There is a saying, "it is better to give than to receive." This is missing the point. Giving and receiving are equal in importance. When we are little babies we must receive everything. Does this mean parents are better than babies? It's not a good comparison. How many people would show up at work to give a day's labor if they didn't receive a paycheck? Of course, there are times when we give without receiving, just as there are times when we receive without giving.

If you don't feel good about yourself, I urge you to do something about it. First, stop feeling bad about yourself. Put up little signs that say, "you are good!" "You deserve the best!" Get out that yellow pad and draw a line down the middle of the page. On the left hand side write, "My good points". On the right hand side write, "My bad points". Then, begin to focus on your good points. Strengthen them. Reinforce them. Reward them. Slowly, they will overpower the bad points. You can also read Psycho-Cybernetics, by Maxwell Maltz. Talk to a psychologist or a psychiatrist if you are having a lot of difficulty with this.

Professionalism

My dictionary defines professionalism as: professional character, spirit, or methods. It's so important to feel and act like a real pro that I want you to spend some time thinking about it. Even if you are not a sports fan, watch one professional baseball game. Why? These guys are amazing. To begin with, they play baseball. Baseball. You know, hit the ball. Run around the bases. Throw the ball. Tag the runner. Score. They play this game so extraordinarily well they earn millions of dollars a year. They are consummate professionals.

How well do you execute your job tasks? Do you give it your best? Or, do you make a half-hearted effort? When you watch a professional baseball game you have the opportunity to see maximum effort in a very open way. When the pitcher throws the ball to the batter, he throws it where the batter can hit it. The object is to throw it so well, however, that the batter will either miss it or hit it poorly. The game is set up to reward excellence. The American system of selling is set up the same way. When you learn the rules, and perform very well, you will win a certain number of games.

When baseball players screw up they flash "error" on the scoreboard. They don't stop the game and beat the guy up. (Although sometimes the fans would like to.) When you make an error, don't make excuses. Don't get bent out of shape. Act like a professional, accept your error, and continue to play the game to the best of our ability. All professionals make errors.

Professionals do everything. They pay attention to every detail. A professional doesn't have serious weakness. This book is loaded with the details that professional sellers are concerned with. There is no skill or idea in this book that you cannot learn to do reasonably well. None. Zippo. Nada. You may not be able to do all of them to same degree of excellence. However, given the time and the effort, you can do all of them without serious weakness. I hope you understand me. This is the essence of what I want to achieve in this book.

Be a pro. Act like it. Feel like it. Take on the spirit of being a top professional seller. It can be fun.

Money

Money is synthetic energy. It was invented by human beings for human beings, and is based 100 percent on the emotion of faith. It has no intrinsic value. Some economists like to think that gold is somehow better than paper. They don't understand. There are people on this earth who wouldn't give you a loaf of bread for a pound of gold. No sir. They want some real money: like seashells.

Money is very similar to real energy, such as electricity or gasoline. It moves things. Give it to a waiter in a restaurant and he or she will move a bunch of food to your table. Like real energy, it has to be stored in a special way. It must be kept in a bank or a strong metal box. If you get too much, too fast, it can act just like a lighting bolt, and burn you or even zap you dead.

The subject stirs up all kinds of emotions. (Probably because it is based on emotion.) Some people have terrible hang-ups about money. Some people think it is the root of all evil. Some worship it. Some people think it is a source of power and influence. The Hunt brothers of Texas inherited a vast fortune from their billionaire father and have practically no influence or power. They seem to be having difficulty just keeping themselves from going broke.

Money is neither good nor bad. It's just this wonderful way we have of keeping track of energy. It is easy to carry, easy to use, and easy to spend. It's so flexible that it's used in most societies, regardless of political form.

Make it fun. Don't let it be a needless source of pain in your life.

Appearance and grooming

Do you like the way you look? I mean do you really like it? Do you feel comfortable in the clothes you wear? I believe you should. When I worked for a large sales organization they made me wear a cheap suit. Their logic was that it made me look more professional. That's a bunch of baloney. A cheap suit looks exactly like a cheap suit. When I went out on my own I began wearing designer jeans and shirts and my income went up.

It is important that you feel comfortable in the clothes you hang on your body. This is work, you know. There is physical comfort as well as psychological comfort. In Hawaii, where the climate is warm, they wear a lot of flowered shirts without ties. In New York City, where it gets cold in the winter, they dress in a much more formal way. I work in Southern California, where the climate is mild. I hate to wear suits and ties. They make me feel constricted. But, on those occasions when I do wear a suit, I like a very good suit. I can recognize a good suit very easily. Can you? It doesn't matter whether you are a woman or a man; you are wise to know how you look.

A very successful real estate broker here in Southern California has his agents wear blue jeans and T-shirts because that is the way most of the buyers dress. Sometimes it is very helpful to dress in a fashion that is similar to your buyers. Not only do you want to feel comfortable, you want your buyers to feel comfortable. This is something you get to decide. This is a judgment call. There are numerous good books and magazine articles on the subject of dressing for success.

Grooming has to do with the way you take care of your clothes and your body parts. It always amazes me how a man or woman can pay $500 for a suit and then wear it with wrinkles. I always take my coat off when I drive a car because it wrinkles the coat very badly in the back. Keep your clothes looking pressed and clean regardless of style or price. Keep your shoes and purses polished and shined. If you wear jewelry, keep it cleaned and shined. There is some work and expense to this, so budget for it.

Pay as much as you can afford for your hair. Good hair stylists are worth every dollar they charge. Keep your nails in good shape. Even your skin is important. Brush your teeth. Everything about you needs some attention. Remember, the professional pays attention to details. You will look good, and and, I promise, you will feel good.

Studying

"Some people regard discipline as a chore. For me, it is a kind of order that sets me free to fly."

Julie Andrews

I hope I have convinced you of the need for study, practice, and training. There is a terrible and serious misconception that good sellers don't need this. This not only hurts individuals, it hurts our entire profession.

Begin by preparing yourself to study. You will need a suitable desk or table, and a really good chair. You can get good chairs at office supply stores for $50 to $100. Your back really needs support, so do not skimp here. Buy notebooks, yellow pads, 3 x 5 cards and pens. Get a bulletin board, or an "action" board.

Set aside money for books, magazines, and seminars.

Make it easy to study. Make it a highly visible activity in your life. Make a commitment to your career. Selling techniques and market conditions are constantly changing. Why wake up one day in 20 years and regret your lack of income because you failed to study? The pain of regret weighs tons. The pain of discipline weighs ounces.

Ethics

Good and bad, right and wrong are matters of personal values. I can't decide these things for you. I can only decide them for me. You may not even feel they are important, but I do.

Benjamin Franklin once said that honest is the best policy. I agree with that. I agree with it now, more than ever. There are people who believe that you have to lie in order to make sales. They are fooling themselves. I refuse to lie, and my productivity us usually in the top ten percent. Dr. Toni Grant is a well-known psychologist and the pioneer of psychology on the radio. She says that people lie because they are afraid. So, if you believe you have to lie to make sales, what are you afraid of?

Let me give you some purely practical reasons for telling the truth. Lying clutters up the memory. It takes a lot of thinking energy to keep track when you start to spin a web of lies. When talking to a client I don't have to worry about what I said last time we spoke. I just have to speak the truth. It's easier that way. I earn respect because my clients know I am going to tell them the truth. They don't always like it, but they respect it. Repeat business is another reward. Because I am truthful my customers come back to me. They refer their friends and associates to me. I don't know about you, but that make me feel good inside.

If you are considering coming into this profession, I urge you to bring your integrity with you. We need it. This profession is what we make it. I think it's pretty good. I also believe there is room fro improvement. The way this is going to happen is through our deliberate effort to encourage the best ethical practices we know.

Work Habits

Habits are very powerful. We hear of the *force* of habit. Well, that is a very accurate description. We are all creatures of habit. This is very noticeable when you look at how we get up in the morning. We usually develop a very predictable routine. And, when something interrupts that routine, we really feel it. I always start with a shower. When I can't take my shower, first thing, I am very, very aware of it. Some people have to have a cup of coffee. Some people must have breakfast. Some people need to take a walk. It's a habit. It no longer requires active thought.

So, think how powerful it is to have a good set of work habits. As you re-read this book, and see the skills and topics that you desire, think you how you can make them habits. That way, once you learn them, they can be integrated permanently into your routine. They will begin to take care of you, instead of you having to spend time taking care of them. Doesn't that sound like a god deal?

Manners

This is about politeness, courtesy, and graciousness. I once read the complaint that manners were just a lot of falderal and needless words. A wise diplomat responded by agreeing that it's true. But he pointed out that the air in an automobile tire is needless too, however, it makes the ride smooth, and so much more pleasant.

What kind of a ride do you want to give your buyers? Is it smooth and pleasant? Or do you want to give them a rough go? I like to make it very easy for buyers to say no to me. With a little effort, I make it even easier for them to tell me yes.

Please, and *thank you*, are still quite effective words. Use them. People who are polite and gracious are respected for it. I recently visited the Huntington Library where they have a letter that George Washington wrote to his uncle. It began, "Dear Uncle, Please forgive this intrusion on your valuable time..." What a gracious beginning! Here you have the father of our country, the first president, and one of our greatest military generals. This is not a wimp. This is a powerful, intelligent, and wise person.

We all learn the manners and customs of our peers because we grow up with them. But, if you want to grow as a person and expand your horizons, you will need to learn the manners and customs of other. Observation is a very effective way to do this. You can also go ask someone. There are plenty of excellent books and seminars on the subject.

Attitude

Many years ago I attended a seminar called Adventures In Achievement, by E. James Rohn. It was one of the most helpful in my career. I want to share with you one thing from that seminar that had a tremendous impact on my life. It was one of the things that hit me like a ton of bricks. He said, "In order things to change, you have to change. Otherwise, it isn't going to change." Now, you must understand, I wanted things to change I a very big way. It wasn't that I was unhappy with my life. But, I was nearly 30 years old and I wanted to do things with my life that required me to become a better person. That is when I began working on me. The first thing I had to change was my attitude.

This book has 50 topics. It takes years to develop all the skills listed on these pages. So, what can you do Monday morning that will make a difference? Answer: very little. Therefore, I recommend the first thing to work on is your attitude. You know in your heart what you want. Decide right now that your attitude is going to be that you deserve it and you will get it. Make your attitude one of determination. You get to choose your attitude. There is only one thing you can completely control in this life, and that is your own mind. You can't control your customers, your family, the weather, the competition, or the IRS. However, you can completely control your own mind.

Take charge. It may not be easy. There will be setbacks. But, by *believing* you will do it, you will do it. This is where you can begin. And what a beginning. You now know what selling is. Selling is exchanging. You can do that. The mystery is over. That's why I have written this book. You don't have to sit around and wait for the right job, the right manager, or the right product. Go back through this book and start doing what needs to be done in your own judgment.

I can't promise that you will be a great seller. I can't even promise you will be good seller. But, I can promise that you will become a better seller.

www.ingramcontent.com/pod-product-compliance
Lightning Source LLC
Chambersburg PA
CBHW071622170426
43195CB00038B/2037